Running SAP® on Microsoft® Azure

Bert Vanstechelman

Thank you for purchasing this book from Espresso Tutorials!

Bert Vanstechelman
Running SAP® on Microsoft® Azure

ISBN: 978-3-945170-81-6

Editor: Karen Schoch

Cover Design: Philip Esch

Cover Cartoon: Wouter Van Ghysegem

Cartoons in Book: Wouter Van Ghysegem

Interior Book Design: Johann-Christian Hanke

1st Edition 2019, Gleichen

URL: *www.espresso-tutorials.com*

Feedback
We greatly appreciate any feedback you may have concerning this book. Please send your feedback via email to: *info@espresso-tutorials.com*.

Table of Contents

Introduction

SAP will be stopping support for SAP ERP in 2025. Businesses requiring support from SAP will have to be migrated to S/4HANA by then. S/4HANA runs exclusively on SAP HANA. SAP HANA is SAP's in-memory database technology and is designed for high performance. All data is compressed and kept in-memory, which allows read operations to be performed on massive data volumes without accessing disk, thereby avoiding input/output (I/O) bottlenecks altogether.

SAP HANA is only supported on certified hardware. This sounds limiting at first, but it actually isn't. The list of certified hardware is extensive and is growing day by day.

But how do you determine the amount of resources you need? The choice of hardware resources is a balance between adequate performance and acceptable cost. Proper hardware sizing is complicated, but it is important and should not be neglected. There are many things to consider, and in greenfield projects, assumptions need to be made. Growth is never measured correctly. It is either underestimated, which results in business users complaining, hardware needs to be upscaled or, worse, replaced before the end of its life, or, it is overestimated, which means money being wasted, thereby translating into excessive TCO (total cost of ownership).

The introduction of SAP HANA may have intensified it, but the same old question arises—what do you need to run your environment properly? The answer to this question is what keeps many Chief Information Officers (CIOs), SAP administrators and consultants awake at night. Wouldn't be great if you could have an endless amount of hardware at your fingertips? I have seen many cases in which capacity planning went wrong, or the customer ordered too little or too much hardware. With the Cloud, hardware sizing and capacity planning are just a bad memory.

The Cloud comes in several different forms:

- IaaS—Infrastructure as a service
- PaaS—Platform as a service
- SaaS—Software as a service

In this book, we focus on IaaS. When talking IaaS, SAP is supported on Amazon, Google, IBM and many others. Microsoft has a very compelling cloud solution called Azure. Throughout this book, we clarify why migrating to the Cloud makes perfect sense and why we consider Microsoft Azure to be a valuable option both for companies that plan on running an SAP ERP system for the next few years, and for businesses that are moving to S/4 HANA in the near future.

Why should you consider Microsoft Azure?

1. Businesses that have not yet migrated from traditional databases to SAP HANA will have a lot of learning to do. The advantage of Azure is that you can easily deploy SAP HANA-certified systems for your proof of concept, without the need to acquire certified hardware. These systems can be provided in a matter of hours or days. Obtaining, assembling and connecting new hardware in an on-premise setup could take weeks.

2. Organizations can decide to go full cloud or they can opt for a hybrid solution, in which non-production systems run in the Cloud while production systems remain on-premise. This setup is completely transparent from an SAP perspective.

3. Size does not matter. In Azure, you can host production Online Transaction Processing (OLTP) databases on virtual machines with a memory size up to 3.8 terabytes (TB). Customers who need extended memory sizes can utilize Azure Large Instance systems. A Large Instance system is on purpose-built hardware, supporting up to 20 TB of RAM for OLTP "scale up" systems, and 60 TB of RAM for Online Analytical Processing (OLAP) "scale out" systems.

4. New technology is constantly being deployed in the Azure data centers. The hardware renewal rate is always faster than can be achieved in a local data center. You always run your SAP systems on the latest hardware!

5. Microsoft and SAP have a strong partnership, and Microsoft Azure is an SAP S/4 HANA-certified cloud environment. Don't forget that Microsoft itself runs SAP on Azure!

6. And last but not least, in Azure you can optimize your TCO by paying only for what you use.

Content

This book introduces you to the specifics of deploying and maintaining SAP on Azure. It does not attempt to replace the official documentation from SAP and Microsoft. That would be futile. There are over 1000 pages of documentation available at the Azure documentation portal, which is being updated constantly. The goal of this book is to introduce you to the concepts and capabilities of Azure in relation to SAP.

We start our adventure in Chapter 1, where we explain what it is all about and why you should take an interest. We also explain the differences between on-premise, IaaS, PaaS and SaaS.

In Chapter 2, we dive into the world of Azure. Azure is probably the largest data center in the world. In this chapter, we explain concepts such as regions, locations, data centers, availability zones and sets, accounts, computing, storage, and network resources.

In Chapter 3, we discuss how to translate an existing SAP landscape into Azure using the capabilities discussed earlier. The size of the virtual machines, the selection and configuration of the storage, and the network configuration have a significant impact on your SAP environment's performance.

High availability and disaster recovery are like insurance policies—being prepared for the "what if". As with any insurance policy, you need to balance the cost against the event you want to protect yourself from. The more coverage, the more protected you are, but the more expensive the policy becomes. Chapter 4 focusses on Azure's high-availability and disaster-recovery concepts.

SAP is available in combination with different databases and operating systems. In Chapter 5, we highlight the implementation guidelines for every database and operating system supported by SAP and Azure.

In Chapter 6, we outline design guidelines for performance, security, availability and recoverability, and cost savings.

Chapter 7 and Chapter 8 explain how to undertake your migration to the Cloud. SAP is business-critical for many companies; therefore, a lot of things need to be taken into account when migrating to the Cloud.

In Chapter 9, we cover a customer who migrated their SAP environment to the Azure Cloud. We discuss their reasoning and business case to go for a cloud solution. We also describe how they mapped their current infrastructure to the Cloud, taking the Azure capabilities into account, and how they implemented high-availability and disaster recovery.

Last but not least, we wrap it all up in Chapter 10's conclusion.

Acknowledgments

The first person I want to thank is Wouter Van Ghysegem who is the creator of the cover and every cartoon in the book. This is not my first book and probably not my last. For this book, I wanted to combine the serious with the funny.

My gratitude also goes to my colleagues at Expertum. We are a fast-growing company and have more than a century of combined SAP experience between us. Our reference list of SAP implementation projects is amazing.

Finally, and most importantly, I want and need to thank my family and especially my wife, Ilka, who supported me in the writing of yet another book.

My most sincere thanks also go to Alice Adams of Espresso Tutorials for her advice and support and to Karen Schoch who edited the manuscript until it was perfect.

We have added a few icons to highlight important information. These include:

Tips

Tips highlight information that provides more details about the subject being described and/or additional background information.

Attention

Attention notices highlight information that you should be aware of when you go through the examples in this book on your own.

Finally, a note concerning the copyright: all screenshots printed in this book are the copyright of SAP SE. All rights are reserved by SAP SE. Copyright pertains to all SAP images in this publication. For the sake of simplicity, we do not mention this specifically underneath every screenshot.

1 What is it all about?

The number of organizations embracing a cloud-based model is increasing rapidly, whether it be a hybrid or full cloud solution. There are a number of IaaS cloud providers, including Amazon and Google. Microsoft Azure combines traditional computing, storage, and networking (IaaS) with services including databases, analytics, mobile applications, and many more SaaS solutions.

Do you speak IaaS, PaaS or SaaS? Sounds confusing, doesn't it?

Before we continue, let us explain the different cloud offerings (see Figure 1.1):

- In an IaaS model, a cloud provider provides infrastructure traditionally found in a data center, including hosting, cooling, power, servers, storage, and networking. These components are hidden from consumers by a hypervisor or virtualization layer. Many cloud providers offer additional services such as detailed billing, monitoring, security, load balancing and clustering.

- PaaS is in between IaaS and SaaS. While IaaS only provides infrastructure, PaaS provides software developers with a preconfigured development environment. Developers no longer have to worry about system administration, performance, load balancing and high availability. The disadvantage of PaaS, however, is that the company developing the software becomes completely dependent on the PaaS provider. Migrating applications from one PaaS solution to another is not easy; in fact, let's say it's impossible. The advantage of PaaS is that it provides middleware and databases, enabling developers to focus on their applications instead of the underlying infrastructure. PaaS is, in most cases, billed per developer or user, on a monthly basis.
- Applications developed in PaaS can easily be offered in a SaaS model, which is the next layer. In SaaS, applications are installed in the Cloud and are no longer on end users' computers. This means that the application is available from any device. Most SaaS models are subscription based. You pay per user, per month. This is perfect from a budgetary perspective because you always know what to expect. Costs can easily be estimated depending on the growing number of users. Another advantage of SaaS is that the application is maintained by the cloud provider. The latest version of the application is always available. The disadvantage lies in the model itself; everybody uses the same version of the application. There is very little room for customization. Also note that software upgrades are always pushed from the provider to the customer (for example, every quarter). On one hand, you always work with the latest version. On the other hand, end users might arrive in the office and suddenly notice a new version of the business application. No need to spell out that this might lead to confusion, mistakes, frustration and an overloaded helpdesk.

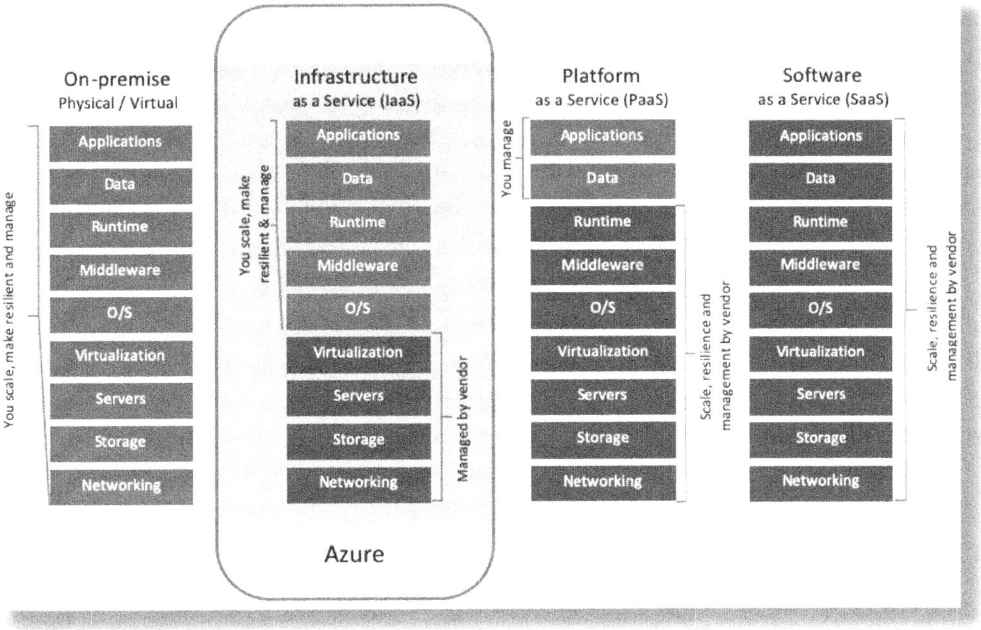

Figure 1.1: On-premise, IaaS, PaaS and SaaS infrastructure stack

1.1 Private or public cloud?

There is a lot of confusion when it comes to the private or public cloud, and the terminology can be intermingled, even in professional publications.

A *private cloud* is a virtual environment dedicated to one customer. The hardware can be installed on-premise or in a remote data center managed by a service provider. The advantage of a private cloud is that the customer has full visibility of what is running where. Hardware resources can be divided and assigned as needed. The disadvantage is that the size of a private cloud is limited to the hardware dedicated to the hypervisor. The number of resources is limited, and when they are all used up, that's it, there's no more. When further resources are required, extra hardware needs to be bought, installed, and connected to the virtual environment.

A *public cloud* is a virtual environment which is shared by many customers. The infrastructure is installed in a remote data center and managed by a service provider. As a customer, you have no visibility of the underlying hardware infrastructure. You assign resources to your virtual machines and it is up to the hypervisor to allocate them and, if needed, move your virtual machine to a server with sufficient free resources. In theory, the advantage of a public cloud is an unlimited amount of resources. When the virtual environment reaches full capacity, it is up to the service provider to add hardware. In most cases, adding or upgrading hardware takes place without customers even knowing about it.

To avoid confusion, we have listed the deployment options in Table 1.1. Bare metal, probably the oldest installation option, can be deployed on-premise or in a remote data center. The systems can be maintained by the customer or by a service provider. This option still remains, and will remain for many years to come. The same goes for a private cloud such as VMware or Hyper-V. With the public cloud, you always deploy with a cloud provider such as Azure or AWS. As with the other installation options, the environment can be maintained by the customer or by a service provider.

Deployment options	On-premise	Remote data center	Cloud provider (Azure, AWS, Google)
Bare metal	Yes	Yes	No
Private cloud	Yes	Yes	No
Public cloud	No	No	Yes

Table 1.1: Different deployment options

1.2 Why should you concern yourself with the Cloud?

Everybody is yelling "cloud" these days, sometimes without a clue what it's all about. A recent study revealed that 70% of all CIOs are considering the Cloud and will implement some form of cloud solution in their company in the near future. So, what are the advantages of the Cloud that has everyone so excited? And, what are the disadvantages that everyone seems to be neglecting?

1.2.1 Capacity planning

What do we need to run our environment properly? The choice of hardware resources is a balance between adequate performance and acceptable cost. Proper hardware sizing is important; it is complicated, but it should not be neglected. There are many things to consider, and in greenfield projects, assumptions need to be made. Growth is usually measured incorrectly. It can be underestimated, resulting in business users complaining, or hardware needing to be upscaled or replaced before the end of its life. It can also be overestimated, leading to money being wasted and an excessive TCO.

In some environments, resources are only needed temporarily; for example, during month-end or year-end processes, or, in retail, during the holidays or in the weeks leading up to Valentine's Day. The advantage of the Cloud is in the possibility for upscaling and right-sizing. You only need to allocate the resources you need, and then increase or decrease as you go.

1.2.2 Agility and elasticity

When it comes to SAP implementations or projects, it can take months before management finally makes a decision. But when they do, all hell breaks loose, and they want to go faster than humanly possible; the new solution has to be up and running yesterday!

Later, there is disappointment if additional hardware is needed. It takes time to communicate with hardware providers and select the most suitable vendor. Once an order is placed, it can take six to eight weeks before the new hardware arrives. It then needs to be assembled, connected to the network, and installed. The new SAP solutions must also be installed, customized to business requirements, and released into production.

In the Cloud, a new development system, training system, or sandbox system is just a button away (a *sandbox environment* is a copy of the current production environment). A new SAP landscape can be deployed in minutes, rather than weeks.

An additional advantage is that you only pay for what you use. What if the system is no longer needed? Just shut it down and be done with it. This is definitely not the case with purchased hardware. Can you imagine shipping your hardware back to the vendor when it is no longer needed? I sure can't.

1.2.3 High availability and disaster recovery

High availability means that when there's a problem with the primary system, a secondary system can immediately take over, with little down time and no loss of data. In most cases, this is an automated process.

The difference between high availability and disaster recovery is that the former is used to protect the application and database from a hardware failure, and the latter is used to protect against a disaster at data-center level. High availability restarts the application as fast as possible on the secondary node, whereas disaster recovery recovers and restarts all applications in a secondary data center.

Traditionally, high availability and disaster recovery result in large standby systems sitting idle most of the time. Businesses with very high requirements go one step further and operate a remote data center as a failover solution should the worst of the worst occur.

Even in the Cloud, you need to consider high availability and disaster recovery. Remember that an IaaS cloud provider basically provides you with compute and storage resources. It is up to you to configure them as needed. Thanks to the capacity, agility and elasticity discussed earlier, you can configure a minimal standby environment to which data is synchronized. The standby environment only needs to be increased to full capacity when required—during disaster recovery, a rehearsal, or a real failover. This has a positive impact on the cost of maintaining such a fallback environment. In addition, many cloud providers have data centers all over the globe; something which is difficult to achieve for companies that are not in the IT industry.

1.2.4 Show me the money!

It is a misconception that the public cloud is always less expensive than bare metal or a private cloud. It might be, but only if you use the public cloud in a smart way. In some cases, on-premise might be cheaper. The Cloud has to be used to its full potential before it becomes less expensive.

Some things to consider:

- Capacity planning—this is difficult in an on-premise environment. You can oversize or undersize, so you have too much or too little. The same applies to a private on-premise cloud. Agreed, it is a cloud which makes it easier to divide resources, but it is still limited to the amount of hardware you have in your data center.
- Agility and elasticity—increasing capacity or enabling new systems are just a button away in the Cloud. This level of agility can never be achieved in an on-premise environment. In addition, you only pay for what you use. The public cloud is very attractive because non-essential systems can be shut down during non-business hours. De-allocating or "snoozing" virtual machines can lead to tremendous cost savings. For example, in a pay-as-you-go model, running your SAP Sandbox systems for ten hours a day, five days

a week, instead of 24/7 would reduce your costs by approximately 70%.

- High availability and disaster recovery are expensive. In an on-premise solution you need standby systems at full capacity, all the time. In addition, the cost of operating a secondary data center, which is distant from the primary data center, should not be underestimated, let alone the network connection between the two. In the public cloud, you only pay for what you use. The cost can be optimized by configuring a small standby environment, only increasing it when needed.
- Hardware renewal—benefit from the latest hardware! New generation processors and storage are constantly being made available. In an on-premise setup, hardware is mostly kept for three to five years.
- Last but not least—compliancy. Many businesses require their data center to be ISO compliant. ISO certifications are expensive to achieve and maintain. In the public cloud, this responsibility is outsourced to the cloud provider and the cost is shared among the many customers using the data centers.

1.3 What about SAP?

There is a lot of confusion when it comes to SAP and the Cloud. In my opinion, SAP is somewhere between PaaS and SaaS.

1.3.1 SAP Cloud Platform

SAP Cloud Platform (SCP) is a PaaS solution offered by SAP to create, operate and extend applications in a secured cloud computing environment. It is managed directly by SAP. SCP is built on the SAP HANA database and can connect to on-premise and cloud-based systems, SAP or non-SAP. SCP uses open standards such as Java, JavaScript and Node.js. SAP Cloud Platform is based on open source technology, developed and supported in partnership with SUSE. SAP has also partnered with Apple to create software development kits which enable you to develop mobile applications for iOS.

SAP Cloud Platform has many capabilities, the most popular are: SAP Fiori Cloud, Forms by Adobe, Rapid Application Development by Mendix, Platform Integration Tools, Data Provisioning, Predictive Services, Leonardo, Internet of Things, Identity Authentication and Provisioning, Mobile Applications, and SAP HANA as a service.

There is an SAP Cloud Platform Developer Edition to get you started. It offers developers an easy and free way to explore SCP and its capabilities.

1.3.2 S/4HANA in the Cloud

S/4HANA is available in two SaaS offerings: the S/4HANA multi-tenant edition and the single-tenant edition. Both options are highly standardized. The fundamental difference is that the multi-tenant edition is shared among many customers and the tenants are automatically upgraded four times a year. It is the most straightforward edition and delivers the best TCO. With the single-tenant edition, upgrades are not automatically pushed, and are done in consultation with the customer. Customizations are possible, but are limited.

SAP also offers S/4HANA in an IaaS setup. The system is deployed in a private cloud in the SAP data centers, managed by SAP.

Last but not least, S/4HANA can be installed and operated on-premise. This can be done on-premise, in a remote data center, or in a private or public cloud. This is managed by you or a service provider (see Figure 1.2).

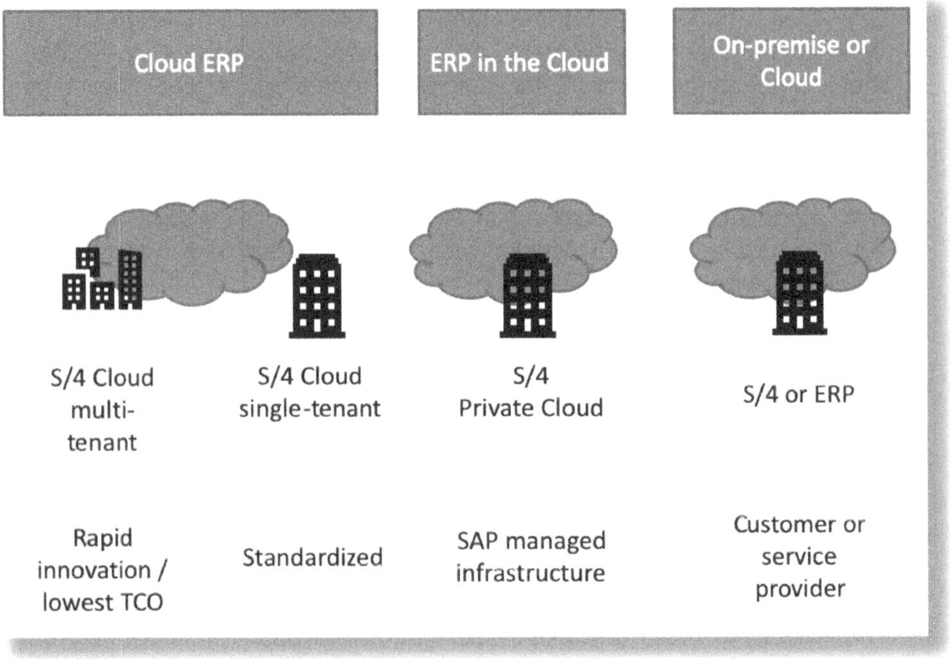

Figure 1.2: SAP Cloud offering

1.3.3 SAP Cloud Appliance Library

SAP Cloud Appliance Library (SAP CAL) is an online library which enables customers to quickly deploy SAP solutions in the Cloud, such as SAP S/4HANA, SAP ERP, and many more. The solutions are pre-configured and ready to use and can be deployed into Amazon Web Services, Microsoft Azure, and the Google Cloud Platform. The only thing you need is an account for your chosen cloud offering. SAP CAL is comparable to the Internet Demonstration and Evaluation System (IDES) that SAP previously offered its customers. While IDES was limited to SAP ERP, SAP CAL covers many more SAP solutions.

1.3.4 Other SAP applications

SAP has many other business applications which are offered in a SaaS model, such as Ariba, SuccessFactors, Fieldglass, etc.

2 The world according to Microsoft!

Welcome to the largest data center in the world! In this chapter, we explain concepts such as regions, locations, data centers, availability zones and sets, accounts, compute, storage and network resources.

2.1 Regions, locations and data centers

Microsoft does not reveal the locations of their data centers for obvious security reasons. As a customer, you can only select a region, such as West Europe, North Central US, or South India. Azure is available in 42 regions around the world, with plans announced for 12 additional regions.

A *region* is a set of data centers in close proximity, connected by a high-performance network. Regions are grouped in geopolitical areas, which ensures data residency, sovereignty and compliance. They allow customers with specific data-residency and compliance requirements to keep their data and applications close. For example, the geopolitical area for Germany is designed to meet the strictest EU data protection rules, under the German Data Trustee act. For most geopolitical areas in the world, Microsoft has at least two Azure Regions; for example, in Europe there is North Europe and West Europe. Regions within a geopolitical area are a significant distance apart and are designed to withstand a complete region failure due to natural disasters such as floods, tornadoes or earthquakes, or man-made disasters such as a complete power-grid failure. The data centers are interconnected via a dedicated high-capacity network.

Every region is divided into availability zones (see Figure 2.1). An *availability zone* is a physically separate location within an Azure Region. Each availability zone is made up of one or more data centers equipped with independent power, cooling, and networking. Availability zones allow customers to run mission-critical applications with high availability and low-latency replication.

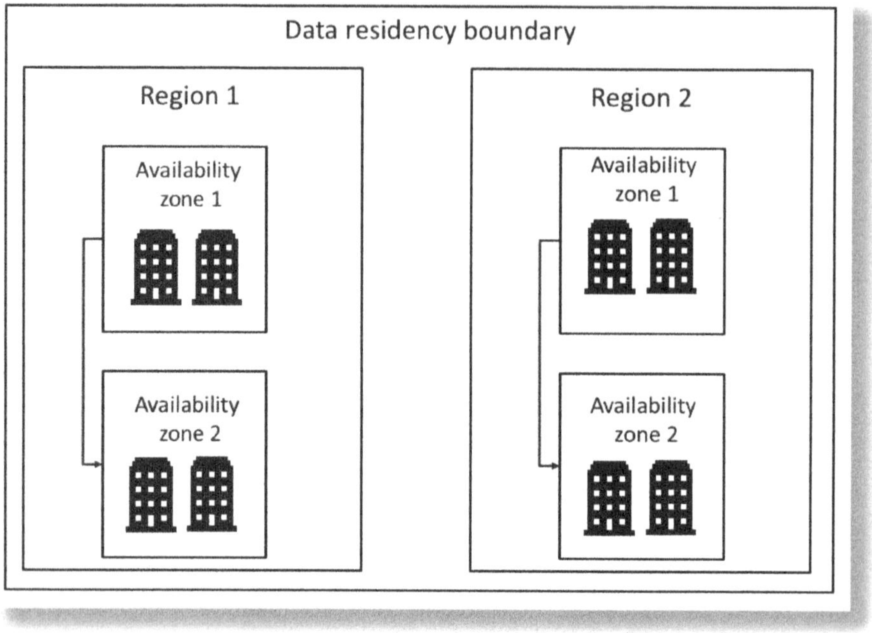

Figure 2.1: Regions, locations and data centers

You should consider the following when selecting a region:

1. **Location**—It does not make sense to deploy your applications in the US when your end user community is located in Europe. It does, however, make sense to divide your applications among different regions if you're operating worldwide. This brings the application close to your end users and guarantees business continuity.

2. **Compliance requirements**—In Germany, for example, the Azure Regions are designed to follow the strictest European Data Protection rules and to adhere to the German Data Protection Act.

3. **Service availability**—Although the situation is changing rapidly, not all Azure services are available in every region. As such, verify whether the services you need are available in the region you are considering.

4. **Data residency and sovereignty**—Keep your applications and data close. This is especially important for European companies which are very sensitive to the location of their data and do not want their data to be replicated outside of Europe.

2.1.1 Paired Regions

Azure is available in multiple geopolitical areas around the world. A *geopolitical area*, according to Azure, is a defined area of the world that contains at least two Azure Regions. A region consists of one or more data centers. Each Azure Region is paired with another region within the same geopolitical area, together making a regional pair (see Figure 2.2). For example, North and West Europe make up a regional pair. As regional pairs reside in the same Azure geopolitical area, both are compliant with any data regulations which might exist within that geographical area.

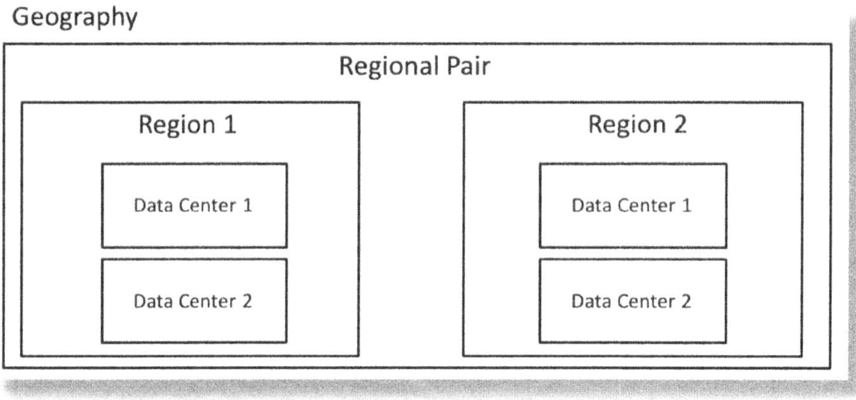

Figure 2.2: Regional pairs

Planned maintenance is done per region. In a regional pair, only one region is updated at a time. In the unlikely event of an outage affecting multiple regions, at least one region in each pair is prioritized for recovery. For most regional pairs, the data centers are located at least 300 miles apart. This reduces the likelihood of natural disasters, civil unrest, or power outages affecting both regions simultaneously.

Azure Regional Pairs can be used to configure business continuity by following these guidelines:

- Configure disaster recovery across regional pairs. When using database replication, deploy the primary and secondary, or standby, database in the paired region. For the application server, provide additional compute resources in the paired region. You can use Azure Site Recovery to keep them synchronized with the primary virtual machines (VMs), (see Figure 2.3). Network availability can be increased by connecting your on-premise data center to both regions using ExpressRoute.

- For applications which support multiple active regions, distribute your systems over regions in the regional pair. This ensures optimal availability and minimizes recovery in the event of a disaster.

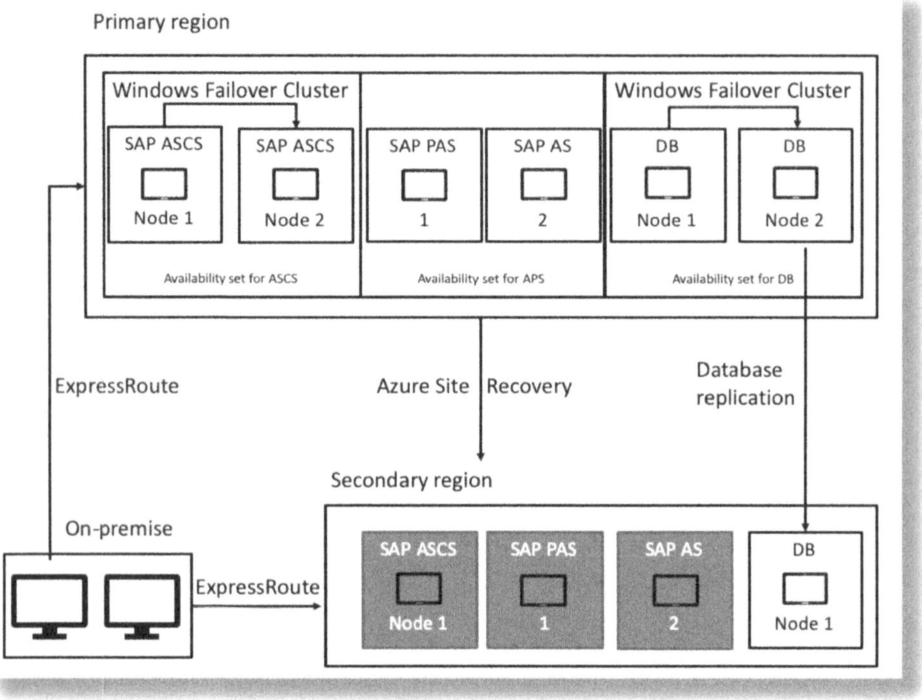

Figure 2.3: High availability using paired regions

What is Azure Site Recovery?

Azure Site Recovery is different to Azure Backup and is not a backup solution. It provides a disaster-recovery solution for both on-premise and Azure virtual machines. Machines are replicated from a primary location to a secondary location. When required, all systems can be started on the secondary location and operated from there. When everything is back to normal, you can fail your machines back to the primary location.

2.2 Accounts, subscriptions and billing

Before you can start working on Azure, you need an account and at least one subscription. A subscription makes a set of resources available to a subscriber and billing location. It is a set of compute, storage, network, and applications or databases. These subscriptions enable companies to divide costs between their different business units (see Figure 2.4). The subscription administrators can provision, start, stop, and delete Azure services, but they can only do so with the services within their assigned subscription. Every subscription has hard and soft limits. The hard limits are set by Azure itself (for example 10,000 VMs per subscription). The soft limits can be set by the Azure administrator. This avoids business units allocating too many resources.

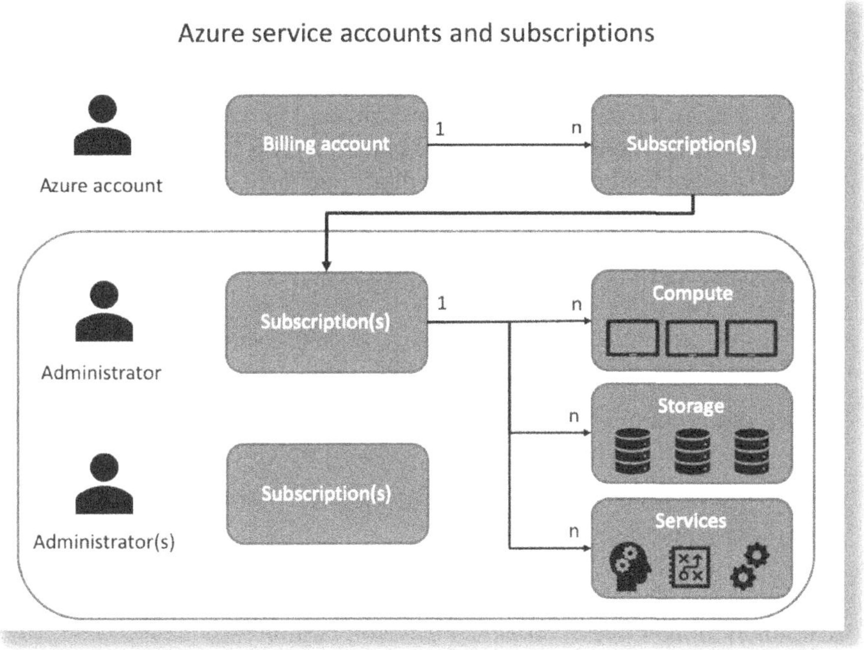

Figure 2.4: Accounts, subscriptions and billing

The Azure account is the same as the billing account. This account has access to the usage data and billing status. The account holder can create, modify and delete subscriptions. These subscriptions can be assigned to the different administrators within the organization. For each subscription, a quota can be set on the amount of resources which can be utilized; for example, compute, storage, databases, applications, and much more.

Subscriptions can be limited

Note that subscriptions can be limited using soft limits. These can be set by the account holder to avoid overallocation (and excessive billing). Subscriptions are also limited using hard limits. These are set by Azure and cannot be changed. For more information see: *https://docs.microsoft.com/en-us/azure/azure-subscription-service-limits*.

2.3 Compute

Microsoft Azure has an endless number of services. But when it comes to SAP, it is all about virtual machines, storage and networking. The list of available virtual machines is huge. Understanding their differences is important in order to choose those that meet your SAP systems requirements and business expectations.

The different VM types are a combination of:

- the amount of memory, virtual CPU's (central processing units) and temporary storage,
- the amount of storage which can be attached and number of IOPS (input/output operations per second) which can be achieved, and
- the number of attached network cards, and bandwidth, which can be achieved.

As mentioned previously, the number of VMs is huge and they are priced according to their specifications. However, note that:

- not all VM's are supported by SAP. Those that are, are listed in SAP Note 1928533—"SAP Applications on Azure: Supported Products and Azure VM types". This note is constantly being updated, whenever VM types are added and removed by Microsoft.

- the difference between the virtual machines is not limited to memory and CPU. Each VM has a different maximum number of disks which can be attached, as well as different storage throughput and network bandwidth. This is very important and should be taken into consideration, especially for large SAP systems.

Virtual machines are divided according to types or series. For example, the Esv3, Ev3, M, GS, G, DSv2, Dv2 series have a high memory-to-CPU ratio and are well suited to relational database servers with medium to large memory requirements.

The following virtual machines are supported by SAP:

- **A-series**—are entry-level virtual machines. They are suitable for sandbox systems, test systems, and development systems only.
- **D-series**—these machines have been in the Azure portfolio for some time. They support traditional SAP workloads. The enhanced version of the D-series is the DS. The DS-series uses premium storage, ideal for I/O intensive workloads that require high performance and low latency. The D-series is ideal for non-production systems. For production systems, the DS-series is a better option. SAP HANA databases are, however, not supported on D-series; the exception is the DS14v2, which is supported for SAP Business One.
- **E-series**—these are virtual machines designed for heavier workloads. The core-to-memory ratio is much higher than on the D-series, making it ideal for applications requiring a lot of memory, such as the S/4HANA Application Servers. As with the D-series, the SAP HANA database is not supported on the E-Series.
- **G-series**—these machines have been available for some time. They are suitable for applications that require faster vCPUs and better temporary storage performance, and which have higher memory requirements. The GS5 was the first VM which was supported for SAP HANA. Unfortunately, the G-series is only suitable for OLAP applications.
- **M-series**—these are currently the largest virtual machines on Azure. The M-series machines go up to 4TB of memory in a single VM. The largest in the series has 128 vCPUs. They are certified for SAP HANA for both OLAP and OLTP workloads.

- **S-series**—these machines are for Azure Large Instances, and are purpose-built. With this series, we leave the virtual world and go back to bare metal. These machines are SAP-certified, supporting workloads from 768GB to 20TB for OLTP in scale-up configurations, and 60TB for OLAP in scale-out configurations.

Accelerated networking

Most virtual machines support accelerated networking. With accelerated networking, all networking policies are applied to the hardware instead of the virtual switch. Applying network policies in the hardware enables the network interface (NIC) to forward network traffic directly to the VM, bypassing the host and the virtual switch, while also maintaining all the policies it applied in the host.

The machines supported by SAP are listed in SAP Note 1928533—"SAP Applications on Azure: Supported Products and Azure VM types". All virtual machines and their capabilities are listed in detail in the Azure documentation portal, which is available at: *https://docs.microsoft.com/en-us/azure/virtual-machines/windows/sizes*.

It is important to refer to both documents when selecting a suitable VM. The SAP note only lists the supported virtual machines and the maximum number of SAPS (SAP Application Performance Standard) they can deliver. The number of SAPS is a hardware-independent and database-independent figure. It is similar to horsepower in the automobile world. Hardware vendors have the tools and procedures to translate the number of SAPS into the hardware resources required. More information is needed for proper hardware sizing. The number of disks, maximum IOPS, and network throughput are also important features to consider when selecting a VM. This type of information is listed in the Azure portal. In Table 2.1, we have combined the information from both SAP Note 1928533 and the Azure documentation portal to provide an amalgamated overview.

VM	VM size	2-tier SAPS	3-tier SAPS	Local SSD	Storage type	# Vdisks	Max. IOPS	Network
A5	2 CPU,4GB	1,500	12,000	135 HDD	Standard	4	4×500	1/moderate
A6	4 CPU, 28 GB	3,000	25,000	285 HDD	Standard	8	8×500	2/high
A7	8 CPU, 56 GB	6,000	50,000	605 HDD	Standard	16	16×500	4/high
A8 / A10	8 CPU, 56 GB	11,000	N/A	382 HDD	Standard	16	16×500	2–4/high
A9 / A11	16 CPU, 112 GB	22,000	N/A	382 HDD	Standard	16	16×500	2–4/very high
D11	2 CPU, 14 GB	2,325	Ask SAP	28 GB SSD	Standard	4	4×500	2/high
D12	4 CPU, 28 GB	4,650	Ask SAP	56 GB SSD	Standard	8	8×500	4/high
D13	8 CPU, 56 GB	9,300	N/A	112 GB SSD	Standard	16	16×500	8/high
D14	16 CPU, 112 GB	18,600	N/A	224 GB SSD	Standard	32	32×500	8/very high
DS11	2 CPU, 14 GB	2,325	Ask SAP	28 GB SSD	Premium	4	8000/6400	2/high
DS12	4 CPU, 28 GB	4,650	48,750	56 GB SSD	Premium	8	16000/12800	4/high
DS13	8 CPU, 56 GB	9,300	91,050	112 GB SSD	Premium	16	32000/25600	8/high
DS14	16 CPU, 112 GB	18,600	Ask SAP	224 GB SSD	Premium	32	64000/51200	8/very high
DS11v2	2 CPU, 14 GB	3,530	Ask SAP	28 GB SSD	Premium	4	8000/6400	2/high
DS12v2	4 CPU, 28 GB	6,680	Ask SAP	56 GB SSD	Premium	8	16000/12800	4/high
DS13v2	8 CPU, 56 GB	12,300	Ask SAP	112 GB SSD	Premium	16	32000/25600	8/high
DS14v2	16 CPU, 112 GB	24,180	Ask SAP	224 GB SSD	Premium	32	64000/51200	8/extremely high
DS15v2	20 CPU, 140 GB	30,430	Ask SAP	280 GB SSD	Premium	40	80000/64000	8/extremely high
GS1	2 CPU, 28 GB	3,580	34,415	384 GB SSD	Premium	4	10000/5000	1/high
GS2	4 CPU, 56 GB	6,900	78,620	768 GB SSD	Premium	8	20000/10000	2/high
GS3	8 CPU, 112 GB	11,870	137,520	1,536 GB SSD	Premium	16	40000/20000	4/very high
GS4	16 CPU, 224 GB	22,680	247,880	3,072 GB SSD	Premium	32	80000/40000	8/extremely high
GS5	32 CPU, 448 GB	41,670	Ask SAP	6,144 GB SSD	Premium	64	16000/80000	8/extremely high

Table 2.1: Virtual machine properties and capabilities

The table is quite straightforward. It lists the VM-type, its maximum capabilities, and the number of SAPS it delivers in two-tier and three-tier configurations.

An outline of the table information is as follows:

- The first column is the VM code. The first letter/s stand for the series, and the numbers represent the type. You can find the same annotation in the Azure portal.
- VM size represents the number of virtual CPUs and amount of memory.
- The third column shows the number of SAPS in a two-tier configuration. In two-tier configurations, you install the database and all SAP components on the same VM in order to avoid network contention. For sizing purposes, refer to the SAPS values in this column of the table.
- The third column shows the number of three-tier SAPS. In three-tier configurations, you install the database on a separate VM and all SAP Application Servers on one or more other VMs. For sizing purposes, refer to the SAPS values in this column of the table.
- The next column indicates the local Solid State Drive (SSD), or non-persistent storage. This depends on the size of the virtual machine and is directly attached to the node. Non-persistent storage should only be used for temporary files, such as the swap space, because it is cleared or re-formatted when the virtual machine reboots or restarts.
- The sixth column lists the storage type required to support the database-related files. There are two types: standard Hard Disk Drive (HDD) and premium SSD. SSD is strongly recommended for the database and transaction log files, especially for large systems.
- The "#Vdisks" column lists the maximum number of disks which can be attached to the virtual machine. This is a very important column because it shows the maximum storage which can be attached to the virtual machine. For example, with a maximum of eight disks and a maximum size of 4TB per disk, you can have a maximum of 32TB for this virtual machine.

- The next column lists the maximum number of IOPS per disk and per virtual machine.
- The last column lists the maximum number of virtual network cards which can be connected, and indicates their maximum throughput.

Non-persistent storage

Non-persistent storage depends on the size of the virtual machine and is directly attached to the node. This should only be used for temporary files, such as the swap space, because it is cleared or re-formatted when the virtual machine reboots or restarts. On Windows, the D drive is a non-persistent drive. This means that the content is lost when the VM is rebooted. On Linux, the drive is mounted at `/mnt/resource`. This temporary storage should be used to save the system paging or swap file.

For SAP HANA

SAP is supported by a wide range of virtual machines: A5-A11, D11-D15, D11v2-D15v2, D2v3-D64v3, E2v3-E64v3, GS1-5, M64s-M128ms. SAP HANA is supported on a selected set of SAP-certified virtual machines for production environments, and on Large Instances, depending on the memory requirements. The supported virtual machines are listed in the SAP Certified and Supported SAP HANA Hardware Directory (see *https://www.sap.com/dmc/exp/2014-09-02-hana-hardware/enEN/iaas.html*). For more information on Large Instances see SAP Note 2316233—"SAP HANA on Microsoft Azure (Large Instances)"

So, you've selected a virtual machine which matches your requirements.

What next? ... Add storage!

2.4 Storage

There are different types of storage available on Azure:

- **Blob**—this is a scalable object store for text and binary data. It is ideal for images, video and audio, for storing backup and restore data, and also for archiving.
- **File**—this is for storing files for distributed access. It enables you to set up a highly available file share. The share can be accessed for read and write from multiple machines.
- **Table**—this Azure table stores large amounts of structured data.
- **Queue**—this is a service to store and receive messages. It is generally used to store lists of messages to be processed asynchronously.
- **Storage**—the Azure Storage consists of unmanaged or managed disks. Disks can be standard type or premium type, depending on the performance requirements.

2.4.1 About blob, file, table and queue storage types

Although the blob, file, table and queue storage types are not frequently used in an SAP context, it is useful to have a basic understanding of them.

Blobs

Blob storage is used for storing massive amounts of unstructured data, such as text or binary data. Blob storage is used for:

- storing documents and images,
- storing and streaming video and audio,
- storing data for backup and restore, and disaster recovery,
- storing archived data, and
- storing huge amounts of data used for data analytics.

Objects in blob storage can be accessed via HTTP or HTTPS. Blobs are also accessible via their URLs (uniform resource locators) from PowerShell, .Net, Java and PHP.

Files

File Storage enables you to set up a highly available network file share (NFS). This share can be accessed in both read and write, allowing virtual machines to access files at the same time. As with blobs, Azure Files can be accessed from anywhere in the world using a URL.

Tables

Table storage stores large amounts of structured data. Azure tables are ideal for storing structured, non-relational data.

Table storage is commonly used for:

- storing TBs of structured data capable of serving web scale applications,

- storing data that doesn't require complex joins, foreign keys, or stored procedures, and that can be denormalized for fast access,
- quickly querying data using a clustered index, and
- accessing data using OData (open data) protocol and LINQ (language-integrated queries) with WCF (Windows Communication Foundation) Data Service .NET Libraries

Queues

Queues are used to send and retrieve messages. The source system/application puts a message in the queue and the target system/application retrieves the message from the queue. A queue can contain millions of messages. Queues are generally used to store lists of messages to be processed asynchronously.

2.4.2 Storage accounts

An Azure storage account contains all of your Azure storage data objects—blobs, files, queues, tables, and disks. Data in your Azure storage account is durable, highly available, secure, massively scalable, and accessible from anywhere in the world over HTTP or HTTPS.

By default, storage accounts are protected by local redundancy. Local redundancy is equivalent to three copies of the same data within the same data center. This can be extended to zone-redundant storage protection, meaning that data is duplicated to another Azure zone. Geo-redundant storage improves this even more by duplicating data between continents. Zone storage and geo-redundant storage are only available for standard storage. Read-access redundant storage allows data to be available in read mode at the secondary location (see Table 2.2).

Replication strategy	Local-redundant Storage	Zone-redundant storage	Geo-redundant storage	Read-access redundant storage
Data is rep-licated across multiple data centers	No	Yes	Yes	Yes
Data can be read from the secondary location	No	No	No	Yes
Number of copies	3	3	6	6
Storage type	Standard & Premium	Standard	Standard	Standard

Table 2.2: Azure replication strategies

2.4.3 Unmanaged vs managed disks

Unmanaged is the original method of managing disk storage. Before you can assign storage to your virtual machines, you need a storage account. A storage account contains all your Azure storage data objects—blogs, files, queues, tables and disks. The VM disks correspond to Virtual Hard Disk (VHD) files, which are stored as page blobs in storage accounts.

Storage accounts have several limitations, such as maximum storage capacity and maximum amount of IOPS. If you require more, you need to create another storage account and divide your storage among them. The limitations make the use of unmanaged disks complicated, especially in SAP environments in which the maximum capacity and number of IOPS have a high impact on the stability of the system. We therefore recommend using managed disks instead.

Managed disks are handled behind the scene. You no longer need to divide the disks among different storage accounts if you exceed limits. Azure handles that for you.

Other advantages are:

- Managed disks take your availability sets into account by ensuring that disks assigned to VMs in an availability set are well isolated in order to avoid single points of failure (see Chapter 4 for more information on availability sets).
- There are always three copies of the managed disks, ensuring a 99.999% availability.
- Managed disks integrate with the Azure Backup Service by providing time-based backups, VM restoration and extensive retention policies.
- Finally, managed disks support snapshotting and encryption.

Because managed disks provide many more capabilities and are easier to handle than unmanaged disks, we strongly recommend using managed disks for SAP environments.

2.4.4 Standard vs premium disks

Depending on the type of SAP workloads you are running, you can choose between standard disks or premium disks:

- **Standard disks**—this storage type is reliable and low-cost, and is great for applications running latency-insensitive workloads. Standard storage is billed depending on the size of the disk and the number of transactions you perform. Standard disks are suitable for non-production systems such as development, acceptance and sandboxes. Standard storage is also available on solid-state drives (SSDs). Standard storage on SSDs offers better latency compared to its HDD counterpart.
- **Premium disks**—this storage type uses SSDs. It delivers high-performance, low-latency disk support for I/O intensive workloads. Using multiple disks, you can attach up to 256TB to a virtual machine. Microsoft highly recommends using premium storage for any

production SAP landscape. Premium storage is billed depending on the size of the disk. The number of transactions has no impact.

Table 2.3 compares the different Azure disk types.

Disk Type	Premium SSD	Standard SSD	Standard HDD
Description	For I/O-intensive workloads. Delivers low latency and high availability.	Designed to provide consistent performance for low IOPS workloads. Delivers better latency compared to HDD disks.	Optimized for low-cost mass storage with infrequent access. Can exhibit some variability in performance.
Workload in an SAP context	SAP production databases	SAP & RDBMS executables, non-production databases	Backup storage & archive files
Max. IOPS	7,500 IOPS provisioned	Up to 500 IOPS	Up to 500 IOPS
Max. throughput	250 MBPS provisioned	Up to 60 MBPS	Up to 60 MBPS

Table 2.3: Azure disk types

2.4.5 Persistent vs non-persistent storage

There are two storage types—persistent and non-persistent:

1. **Persistent storage**. This type of storage, in contrast to non-persistent storage, is not cleared or re-formatted when the virtual machine is started. There are two types of persistent storage—standard and premium storage.

    - What about standard storage? IOPS and bandwidth, or throughput of standard storage, are not provisioned. The performance of the disk depends on the VM type to which the standard disk is attached. You can expect a maximum size of 4TB, an IOPS of 500 and a bandwidth of 60MB/s per disk. For high-performance applications such as SAP, it is recommended to distribute the database among several different disks.

    - Premium storage is built on SSDs. They are very useful for I/O intensive workloads. With premium storage, you can achieve 80,000

IOPS per VM, and a bandwidth of 2,000MB/s per VM. Premium and standard storage can connect to the same VM. This allows you to use premium storage for the database, while using standard (or less expensive) storage for the database dump files.

2. **Non-persistent storage**. This type of storage depends on the size of the virtual machine and is directly attached to the node. Non-persistent storage should only be used for temporary files, such as the swap space, because it is cleared or re-formatted when the virtual machine reboots or restarts.

Using non-persistent storage

On Windows, the D drive is a non-persistent drive. This means that the content is lost when the VM is rebooted. On Linux, the drive is mounted at `/mnt/resource`. This temporary storage should be used to save the system paging or swap file.

2.4.6 Caching

When adding disks to virtual machines, you can specify whether the I/O traffic between the VM and the disks should be cached. Caching exists for both standard and premium storage. Caching makes no sense for operating systems, SAP or RDBMS (relational database management system) binaries. However, for database data and log files, it sometimes does.

Consider the following recommendations when configuring caching for database data and log files:

- Most I/O is a read type. These reads are performance-critical for OLTP applications.
- Writes are in most cases asynchronous and do not hold up user transactions. Writes are performed constantly, except during checkpoints when there is a peak.
- There are hardly any reads in the transaction log or redo files, except during backup and recovery.

- The main load on transaction or redo log files are writes. These are performance-critical because all writes need to be persisted to disk.

Caching should be set to NONE when using standard storage. For premium storage, the recommendation is to use read caching for the data files and 'no caching' for the log files disk.

2.5 Network

Before you can start using your SAP systems in the Cloud, you need some way to connect to them. This is where the networking team comes in. The network configuration needs to be robust, high-performance, and secure. It is therefore recommended to get people with good networking skills on board. In this section, we list the most important building blocks. We consider the network setup to be out of scope of this book. The setup of the network goes beyond SAP. Many businesses run SAP and non-SAP applications. They have interfaces to remote applications, and people working at multiple locations. This all needs to be taken into account when setting up the network and connecting to the Cloud.

2.5.1 Building blocks

The Azure Cloud offers different building blocks to set up and configure the network to, from, and within the Cloud. In this section, we cover the most important of these.

Virtual network

A network consists of connections, linking nodes such as servers, computers, smartphones, and other electronic devices, so that the applications using them can communicate among each another. In the Cloud, the network is, as among all other components such as compute and storage, virtual. Configuring and administering a virtual network is comparable to a physical network, with one exception—there is no need to fiddle with the network-cables, meaning no pulling cables from the router or gateway to the system network card.

In Azure, virtual networks are free of charge. Every Azure subscription is allowed to create up to 50 virtual networks across all Azure Regions. The peering of two virtual networks, either in the same region or in different regions, enables you to route traffic between them. Inbound and outbound traffic is charged at both ends of the peered networks.

Network Security Groups (NSGs) allow you to filter network traffic to and from resources in your virtual network. NSG rules can be defined to allow or deny access to your SAP services; for example, allowing access to the SAP Application ports from on-premise IP address ranges.

Bandwidth

Bandwidth refers to data moving in and out of the Cloud. Data moving into the data center is free of charge. Data moving out is also free as long as you do not exceed the 5GB per month limit, except when using Express-Route.

The Azure Pricing Calculator

The Azure Pricing Calculator is an easy-to-use calculator which assists you in calculating the total-cost-of-ownership of your environment in the Azure Cloud. It is considered the starting point for anyone seriously considering a cloud deployment. For more information visit the calculator at: *https://azure.microsoft.com/en-us/pricing/calculator.*

IP Address

According to Wikipedia, an *Internet Protocol address* (IP address) "is a numerical label assigned to each device connected to a computer network that uses the Internet Protocol for communication". IP addresses are the foundation of computer networks, the Internet and the Cloud.

There are two types of IP addresses—public addresses, used for communication with the Internet, and private addresses, used for communication within a virtual network and on-premise systems.

Firewall

A *firewall* is a network device that monitors and controls all incoming and outgoing network traffic based on predetermined rules. It is typically a barrier between the trusted or private network and the untrusted network or Internet. Azure Firewall is a cloud-based network security service which has the same capabilities as a traditional firewall. It differs from a traditional firewall in that it has built-in high availability, and is scalable depending on the amount of traffic.

Domain Name System (DNS)

The Domain Name System (DNS) is a hierarchical and decentralized naming system for computers, services, and other resources connected to the Internet or to a private network. In human language, the DNS is the phonebook of the Internet. Azure DNS allows you to host your DNS in Azure. Your DNS can be either public or private. A public DNS is open to the Internet, whereas a private DNS is only visible to the virtual machines that are in your private virtual network.

Load balancer

A load balancer does exactly that—it balances the load between two units or more. Load balancers are used in an SAP context for high availability for both the SAP Central Services Instance (SCS) and the database. There are two types of load balancers—basic and standard. Unless you want to deploy your SAP systems across availability zones, the basic load balancers are sufficient. The Basic Azure Load Balancer is free of charge, and the Standard Azure Load Balancer has a charge associated with it.

Active Directory

Active Directory is a directory service developed by Microsoft to be used in the Windows domain. It is used to authenticate users, services and computers. There are several Active Directory offerings in Azure, but the free edition is included with every Azure subscription, and is sufficient for most SAP installations.

Active Directory and Single Sign-on (SSO)

The Azure Active Directory can also integrate with the SAP Cloud Platform (SCP) to provide SSO access to the applications deployed there, such as SAP Analytics Cloud (SAC).

2.5.2 Connecting to Azure

There are several options to connect to the systems that you deploy in Azure. Although you can connect over the public internet, most organizations require a private connection using a virtual private network (VPN) tunnel over the Internet, or a direct dedicated network connection to the Microsoft data center.

There are three possibilities to connect to the Microsoft Azure Cloud:

Point-to-Site VPN or Client VPN

In a Point-to-Site (P2S) VPN, client machines connect directly to Azure through a VPN. Every user has their own VPN connection. They are not routed through the Enterprise WAN (wide area network). This solution is impractical and is only suitable during proof of concept when only a few users need to connect to the SAP systems deployed in Azure. In most cases, it should be disregarded.

Site-to-Site VPN

In this scenario, a VPN connection from a single location in the customer network is used to connect to the systems deployed in Azure. This network traffic routing is transparent for end users, and also on-premise systems, which need to connect to systems in Azure, and vice versa. The Site-to-Site connection is the simplest and most cost-effective type of connection that can be deployed. The downside is that you use a shared internet path. There are no guarantees regarding throughput and latency.

ExpressRoute

While a Site-to-Site VPN uses the Internet, ExpressRoute uses a dedicated connection between the on-premise network and Azure. The private connection is facilitated by a provider. ExpressRoute connections do not go over the public internet. They are more reliable, faster, and more secure than a typical internet connection (see Figure 2.5). Many service providers guarantee an uptime connection and performance Service Level Agreement (SLA). Most providers are able to upscale or downscale the connection throughput as needed.

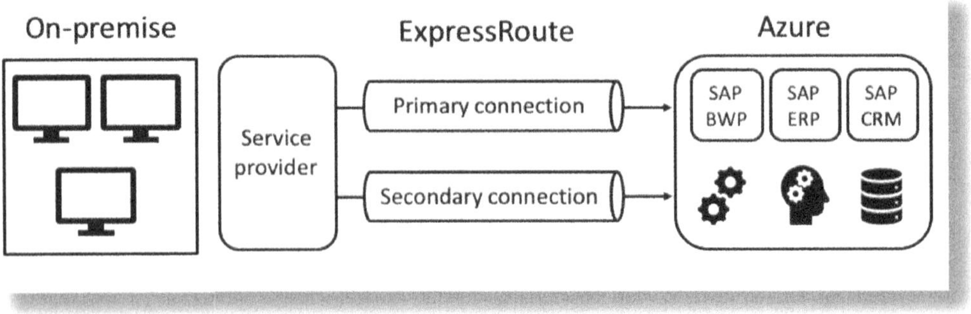

Figure 2.5: Express connection to Azure

Table 2.4 lists the different options to connect to the Cloud. Point-to-Site is not a viable solution due to its high maintenance. A VPN connection needs to be configured on every device used to connect to the Cloud. Most customers choose between Site-to-Site or ExpressRoute. We strongly recommend ExpressRoute when running SAP production systems in Azure because of the guaranteed performance and availability.

Connection	Description	Customer	Segments & workloads
Secure Point-to-Site connectivity	Point-to-Site (e.g., PC to Cloud) Connect from anywhere	Small businesses	Developers Proof-of-concepts Small-scale deployments
Secure Site-to-Site connectivity	Virtual Network (Site-to-Site)	Small to medium-sized businesses (SMBs)	SMB Connect to Azure IaaS and PaaS

Connection	Description	Customer	Segments & workloads
Private Site-to-Site connectivity	ExpressRoute	Large enterprises	SMB & large enterprises Mission-critical workloads Disaster-recovery setups to the Cloud

Table 2.4: Possibilities to connect to the Azure Cloud

2.5.3 Connections and gateways

Three components are needed to connect the on-premise network to Azure: a local network gateway, a VPN gateway and a connection.

Connections

A connection connects two virtual networks—a virtual network and your local network—using Internet Protocol Security (IPsec) or a virtual network to an ExpressRoute circuit. Traffic between the two networks is encrypted by one gateway and decrypted by the other, which protects data transmitted via the Internet.

A connection consists of different components, depending on the connection type:

- When connecting two virtual networks, each connection contains a virtual network gateway. The virtual networks can be in different regions and subscriptions.
- When connecting a virtual network to an on-premise network (also known as a Site-to-Site connection), the connection contains a virtual network gateway for the Azure side of the connection and a local network gateway which represents the on-premise hardware or software VPN device.

Local network gateway

A local network gateway represents the hardware or software VPN device in your local network. The local network gateway contains your public IP address and the network range of your on-premise systems. Use this with a connection to set up a Site-to-Site VPN connection between an Azure virtual network and your local network.

VPN gateway

A VPN gateway is a component used in communications to allow data flows between one network and another. It is used to connect your on-premise network to the virtual network in the Cloud. The connection is secure and uses industry-standard protocols such as IPsec and Internet Key Exchange (IKE). You can use a VPN gateway for connections over the Internet via VPN or ExpressRoute:

- A VPN gateway is used to send encrypted data across the public Internet. Site-to-Site, Point-to-Site and VNet-to-VNet use a VPN Gateway.
- An ExpressRoute gateway is used to send encrypted data across a private connection.

A virtual network can only have one gateway type. For example, you can have a virtual network that uses a VPN gateway and another that uses an ExpressRoute gateway.

- **ExpressRoute gateways**

ExpressRoute gateways come in different options or tiers. The higher the tier, the more CPUs and network bandwidth are allocated to the gateway. As a result, you can achieve a higher network throughput to the virtual network.

ExpressRoute gateways can be of the following types:

- standard
- high-performance
- ultra-performance

You can always upgrade your gateway to a more powerful type. This can be done online, except when upgrading to ultra-performance.

Table 2.5 shows the gateway types and the estimated performances.

Gateway type	Bandwidth uptimes to
Standard SKU	1Gbps
High-Performance SKU	2Gbps
Ultra-Performance SKU	9Gbps

Table 2.5:VPN Gateways for ExpressRoute, types and options

▶ VPN gateways

A VPN gateway is used to connect your on-premise network to your virtual network in Azure. Site-to-Site, Point-to-Site and VNet-to-VNet use a VPN gateway. VPN gateways come in several versions (see Table 2.6). Different workloads require different types of VPN gateways.

Type	S2S/VNet-to-VNet tunnels	P2S SSTP connections	P2S IKEv2 connections	Throughput
Basic	Max. 10	Max. 128	Not supported	100 Mbps
VpnGw1	Max.30	Max. 128	Max. 250	650 Mbps
VpnGw2	Max. 30	Max. 128	Max. 500	1 Gbps
VpnGw3	Max. 30	Max. 128	Max. 1000	1.25 Gbps

Table 2.6: VPN Gateways for internet, types and options

▶ Zone-redundant gateways

Gateways are highly available by default. They can be made zone-redundant. This physically and logically separates them into different availability zones, thereby protecting connectivity from zone-level failures.

Table 2.7 lists the zone-redundant VPN gateways and their capabilities.

Type	S2S/VNet-to-VNet tunnels	P2S SSTP connections	P2S IKEv2 connections	Through-put
VpnGw1AZ	Max.30	Max. 128	Max. 250	650 Mbps
VpnGw2AZ	Max. 30	Max. 128	Max. 500	1 Gbps
VpnGw3AZ	Max. 30	Max. 128	Max. 1000	1,25 Gbps

Table 2.7: Zone-redundant VPN gateways

Table 2.8 lists the zone-redundant gateways for ExpressRoute.

Gateway type	Bandwidth uptimes to
ErGw1AZ	1Gbps
ErGw2AZ	2Gbps
ErGw3AZ	9Gbps

Table 2.8: Zone-redundant gateways for ExpressRoute

3 How to design your landscape?

In this chapter, we discuss how to translate an existing SAP landscape into Azure using the capabilities discussed earlier. The size of the virtual machines, the selection and configuration of the storage, and the network configuration have a significant impact on the performance of your SAP environment.

Making sure that the Cloud matches your expectations is a serious business. Your requirements need to be analyzed step-by-step:

- Create an inventory of your current SAP landscape. Evaluate the CPU, memory and storage use of the existing infrastructure. If possible, try to obtain the number of SAPS. Most hardware vendors have matrices in which they list their servers with the maximum number of SAPS they can deliver. Compare those with the number of SAPS delivered by Azure virtual machines. This information can be found in SAP Note 1928533—“SAP Applications on Azure: Supported Products and Azure VM types”.
- If estimating the number of SAPS of the current infrastructure seems impossible, list the number of CPUs, architecture, speed, and the amount of memory assigned to every SAP instance.
- It is important to consider the maximum number of IOPS your storage is able to deliver. If unknown, tools exist to estimate maximum storage performance.
- Every sizing exercise should include a buffer for growth. This is important in on-premise installations, because extending capacity in those installations is not so easy. We have seen calculations in which a 50% growth for the next five years was included. The buffer for growth should still be considered in a cloud installation. However, unlike on-premise architectures in which it is difficult to add resources, resources can be added as demand increases. The growth figure is therefore less important. It should, however, still be considered, especially when comparing TCO between an on-premise and a cloud installation.
- Changing from a two-tier to a three-tier setup during the conversion to Azure impacts the sizing of the environment. In a two-tier

setup, the SAP Application Server and database share the same system. In a three-tier setup, the SAP Application Server and database each have their own server. Dedicated database SAPS are typically less than 20% of the total number of SAPS.

Did you say "two-tier" and "three-tier"?

What are these tiers all about? If the SAP Application Server and database share the same host, should this not be called "one-tier"? You only have one system? Well, not exactly! SAP consists of three tiers—the presentation layer, application layer and database layer. The presentation layer is always installed on end users' desktops, and as such, two-tier is the minimal server setup.

- While you are redesigning your infrastructure, it is an opportune time to review your business requirements against high-availability and disaster-recovery possibilities. Azure provides many capabilities to improve the Recovery Point Objective (RPO) and Recovery Time Objective (RTO) by using availability sets, zones, and different regions. If implemented cleverly, uptime can be increased without exceeding your TCO.
- Evaluate your performance requirements. Thanks to agility and elasticity, scaling can increase performance on-demand, thereby improving application response time at peak periods.
- Design your network topology; not only the network between the systems in the Cloud but also the connections to your office. Depending on your latency requirements, you can consider connecting through a Site-to-Site VPN using the Internet or a dedicated private connection (ExpressRoute).

3.1 The virtual machine

The list of available virtual machines in Azure is huge, but not all of them are suitable for SAP. Follow the suggested guidelines below to help you select the one which meets your requirements:

- Calculate the SAPS requirement for your SAP system. For existing systems, the SAPS related to your current hardware can often be determined by your hardware vendor, or it can be estimated based on existing SAP benchmarks. New installations, also known as greenfield installations, have to go through a sizing exercise via Quick Sizer.
- SAP developed Quick Sizer to assist customers and consultants with proper hardware sizing. With Quick Sizer, you can translate business requirements into technical requirements. It consists of a questionnaire based on business-related statistics such as how many invoices or sales documents you process per hour. Quick Sizer then calculates CPU, disk, memory, and I/O resource categories based on the throughput number. It also takes into account the number of users working concurrently with the SAP system. The result of this calculation is the number of SAPS, which is independent of hardware and database. You can compare it to horsepower in the automotive world. Hardware vendors have the tools and procedures to translate the number of SAPS into the hardware resources needed.
- On your existing system, estimate the I/O operations per second on the RDBMS server. Operating system tools exist to do this. For new systems, Quick Sizer should also give you a rough idea of the I/O requirements.
- Compare the required number of SAPS and IOPS with what is provided by Azure virtual machines. The number of data disks which can be added to a VM depends on its type. You should calculate the maximum number of IOPS that can be achieved with your preference of VM type.
- The number of SAPS is documented in SAP Note 1928533—"SAP Applications on Azure: Supported Products and Azure VM types. The number of IOPS per VM can be found online in the Azure documentation.

3.2 Storage layout

The disk layout used in on-premise installations is also applicable to the Cloud. From a storage perspective, there is basically no difference between running an SAP system on-premise or in the Cloud

3.2.1 SAP Central Services Instance and SAP Application Servers

The layout for the SAP Central Services Instance (SCS) and SAP Application Servers is straightforward:

The SAP Central Services Instance

The SAP Central Services Instance consists of the message server and the enqueue server. For ABAP-based systems, it is called ABAP SAP Central Services (ASCS). For Java-based systems it is just called SAP Central Services (SCS).

- The SCS hosts the global directory which contains the executables shared among all application servers. It also contains the configuration profiles and stores the log files which need to be accessible from all application servers. The transport directory also resides on the SCS. It is therefore good practice to add a logical volume or drive letter, separate to the operating system or swap disk, in order to store the above. This is necessary so that if the SAP system fills the disk unexpectedly, an operating system crash cannot occur. This could happen if both share the same logical volume or drive letter.
- Managed disks are available with sizes from 32GB to 4TB. Adding two 64GB disks, one for the operating system and another for SAP, is one option. Another option is to use one 128GB disk, splitting it up in several logical volumes or drive letters (see Table 3.1). Nothing is needed for the swap space. Swap is always deployed on the non-persistent disk, which comes by default with the virtual machine selected.

128GB Disk	Logical volume or drive letter	Size	Content
Partition 1	C:	75GB	Operating system
Partition 2	E:	50GB	SAP executables and transport system

Table 3.1: Sample disk layout for the SCS on Windows

- There is nothing business-critical on an SAP Application Server. To be honest, it only consists of a bunch of executables. As such, one disk divided into two partitions—one for the operating system and another for the SAP Application Server—is sufficient.

Use standard HDD or SSD

The Central Service Instance and SAP Application Servers are normally not affected by I/O performance. Therefore, standard HDD or SSD is sufficient. Premium SSD would be overkill.

3.2.2 The database server

The disk layout in the Cloud is comparable to the on-premise installation. The layout for the database server depends on the database technology used. The default layout of an Oracle database is completely different to an SQL Server or MaxDB.

It is recommended to separate the executables of the operating system, RDBMS, and SAP from the database files.

The following are our recommendations for the disk layout on the database server:

- Use one disk which contains the operating system (OS) and all the binaries of the RDBMS. System databases from SQL Server and SAP ASE may be installed on the same disk because they are not used intensively.
- Use several disks for the database data and log files. It is strongly recommended to deploy your database on premium SSDs. If the database IOPS requirements are high, you could consider storage pools (Windows) or striping via Logical Volume Management (Linux).

You should consider the following points when planning your disk layout:

- the layout of your database, the number of data files and their sizes
- the maximum number of IOPS, latency and disk throughput which can be achieved by a single disk
- the maximum number of disks which can be added to the virtual machine
- the overall storage throughput a virtual machine can provide
- VM SLAs

Azure Standard Storage and Azure Premium Storage deliver a different amount of IOPS. I/O latency also differs between the two storage types. Also note that each VM type has a maximum number of data disks that you can attach. In addition, premium storage can only be used with certain VM types.

As a result, deciding on a certain VM type should not only be driven by the CPU and memory requirements, but also by the IOPS, latency and disk throughput requirements.

Use premium storage for the database

Using premium storage is highly recommended for your database data, transaction log and redo files, even for non-production systems.

Figure 3.1 shows an example of a storage layout for a database server. There is one disk for the operating system and RDBMS executables, and a software RAID (redundant array of independent disks) or storage pool of several disks for the transaction log and database files. The software RAID is used to increase the number of IOPS which can be achieved by a single disk. RAID-0 is sufficient because storage is replicated threefold by default on Azure.

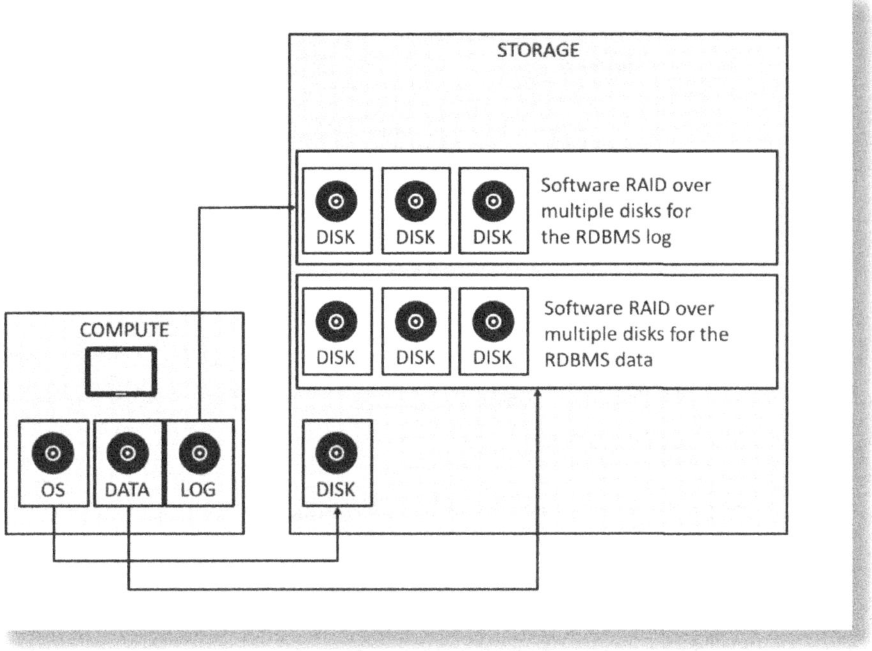

Figure 3.1: Recommended storage layout for the database server

3.3 Autoscale

In the Cloud, you pay as you go. Having the right amount of resources is therefore crucial. This is where Azure Autoscale comes in. It allows you to have the right amount of resources to handle your application load. Resources can be added or removed as needed, saving you money when resources are sitting idle. You specify a minimum and maximum number of instances to run, and add or remove VMs automatically, based on a set of rules (see Figure 3.2). Having a minimum number ensures that your application is always running, even when it's under no load. Setting a maximum number limits your total cost. You can automatically scale between these two extremes using rules you create.

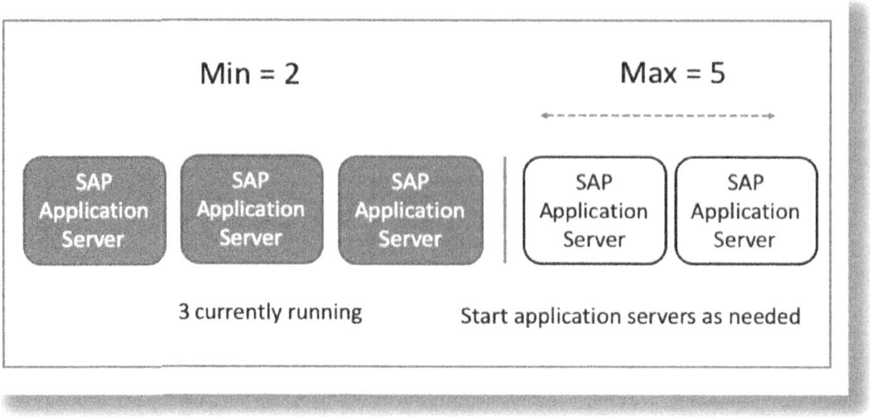

Figure 3.2: Azure Autoscale

When a rule is met, one or more autoscale actions are triggered and VMs can be added or removed.

Rules can be based on metrics or can be time-based:

- Rules based on metrics can be derived from different methods. Some commonly-used statistics include CPU usage, memory usage, thread counts, queue length, and disk usage. For a list of the telemetry data you can use, Autoscale Common Metrics. Custom metrics can be leveraged as well. If you have configured your application(s) to send metrics to Application Insights, you can leverage those metrics to make decisions on whether to scale or not. SAP, by default, does not write any metrics. However, you could use a workaround by monitoring the CPU usage of the work processes.
- An example of a time-based rule is the addition of an SAP Application Server during month-end closing.

For more information on Autoscaling Metrics please visit https://docs.microsoft.com/en-us/azure/azure-monitor/platform/autoscale-common-metrics

3.3.1 Horizontal vs vertical scaling

Scaling can be done horizontally or vertically. *Horizontal scaling*, where you increase or decrease the number of virtual machines, is the most straightforward. Horizontal scaling allows you to run potentially thousands of virtual machines to handle the load. *Vertical scaling* is something different. VMs are not added, but scaled-up or scaled-down by adding or removing memory, CPU and/or disk space. Vertical scaling has some limitations. It is dependent on the availability of larger hardware within the same Azure Region. In addition, virtual machines are divided into scaling pairs. A D1v2 forms a scaling pair with the D5v2. It cannot be scaled up to a G5 or scaled down to a A0. Vertical scaling also usually requires the VM to be stopped and started.

3.3.2 Scaling in an SAP context

Horizontal scaling only makes sense for SAP Application Servers. Running more than one SCS is technically not possible. Apart from the scaled-out SAP HANA system, there is always only one database server. Unfortunately, a scaled-out SAP HANA system cannot handle the automatic addition or removal of instances.

For SAP Application Servers, you can configure a rule in which an additional VM is started when the work processes consume more than 70% of the CPU for more than 30 minutes. The application server would have to be added to the logon group in order for the message server to consider it in the load balancing configuration. This can be done upfront, when the application server is installed. If the application server is not running, it is not considered by the message server.

Removing or deactivating a VM when usage drops below a certain percentage is a little bit more complicated. You first need to remove it from the logon group, wait some time until nobody is connected, and then stop the application server. The logon groups are stored in a database table. You could write a rule which sends an event to SAP to start an ABAP program, or you could write an SQL command which removes the application server from the table, then wait until the next day and shut down the application server.

Vertical scaling requires the VM to be restarted. In addition, adding memory requires the SAP Application Server to be reconfigured. Both these requirements make vertical scaling impractical in an SAP context.

SAP silent installations

Automation is key! You can use the Software Provisioning Manager (SWPM) silent installer to perform unattended installations. This is very useful in disaster recovery and on-demand scaling scenarios in which systems need to be deployed automatically. You can save time by leveraging these techniques and setting up a repeatable process, thereby reducing the chance of errors. For further information, see *https://techcommunity.microsoft.com/t5/Running-SAP-Applications-on-the/SAP-S-4HANA-Silent-Installation/ba-p/711289.*

3.4 Hybrid deployment

Although the Cloud is gaining popularity, many customers do not feel comfortable migrating their entire SAP landscapes, especially when it comes to production systems. For system engineers, the thought of no longer being able to run to the data center, and hit or kick the system when it goes wrong, is frightening. Management also feels uncomfortable about no longer having critical business data on-premise. Fortunately, these feelings of uncertainty are fading away fast, because a new generation is entering the scene—a generation who grew up with Facebook, Instagram, and WhatsApp. The younger generation does not care where the data resides, as long as it is always accessible and fast.

A hybrid deployment enables you to install one or more non-production systems in the Azure Cloud while keeping your critical production systems on-premise. Most customers start with the deployment of a sandbox system. Sandbox systems are rarely critical, unless they are used for a project with a strict deadline. Because, in most cases, they are a copy of production, they are considerably large and enable actual business scenarios to be run. They are ideal for testing the functionality of the Cloud.

A hybrid deployment is the implementation of SAP systems in which some systems are deployed in the Cloud, and others remain on-premise. The systems residing in the Cloud can share a common transport directory by being part of the on-premise Microsoft Domain, OpenLDAP and DNS. It basically means having a Site-to-Site VPN or private network connection between the on-premise and Azure systems. Because networking is transparent between the two sites, the SAP systems are unaware that they are not running next to each other (see Figure 3.3).

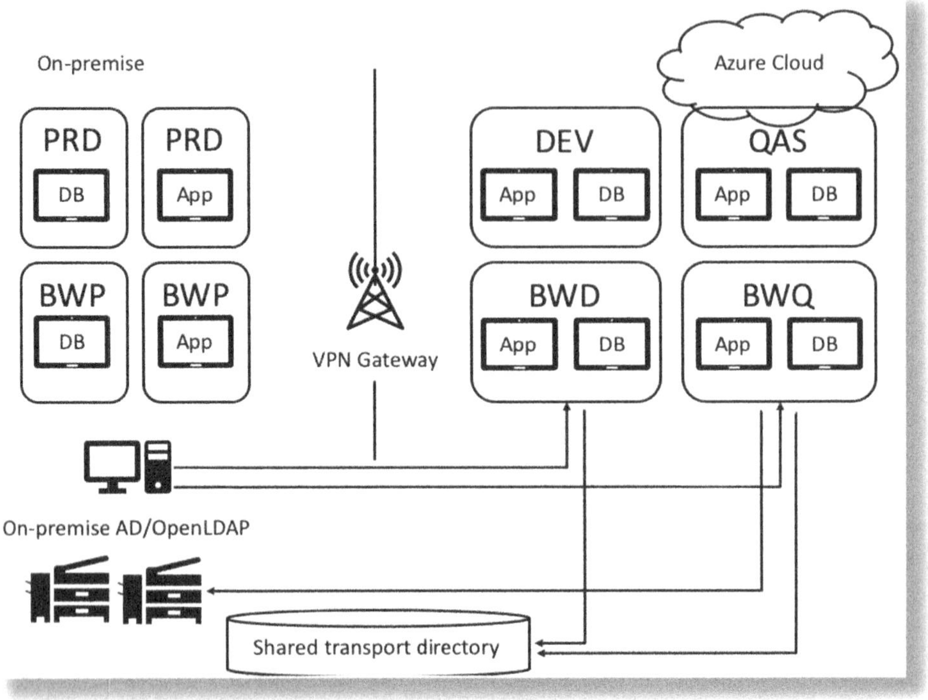

Figure 3.3: Hybrid deployment

With reference to SAP systems, hybrid deployment has some restrictions:

- Running different components of one SAP system at different locations is not supported. The SCS, application servers and database should be deployed either on-premise or in the Cloud. Cross-deployments are not supported. The reason for these restrictions is the requirement for a very low-latency, high-performance network within one SAP system, especially between the application instances and the RDBMS layer of an SAP system.
- Due to network latency, it is also not recommended that you deploy your SAP BW system in the Cloud, but rather keep your SAP ERP or S/4 on-premise. These systems transfer a huge amount of data between each other every day. The same applies to other SAP components such as SAP CRM or SAP SCM. We therefore strongly recommend that all systems within the same tier be installed close together, be it on-premise, at a remote data center, or

in the Cloud. In this context, a *tier* is a group of systems with the same functionality. All development systems are part of the development tier, and all acceptance systems are part of the acceptance tier (see Figure 3.4). The concept of "tier" here has nothing to do with the two-tier or three-tier layout discussion we had earlier.

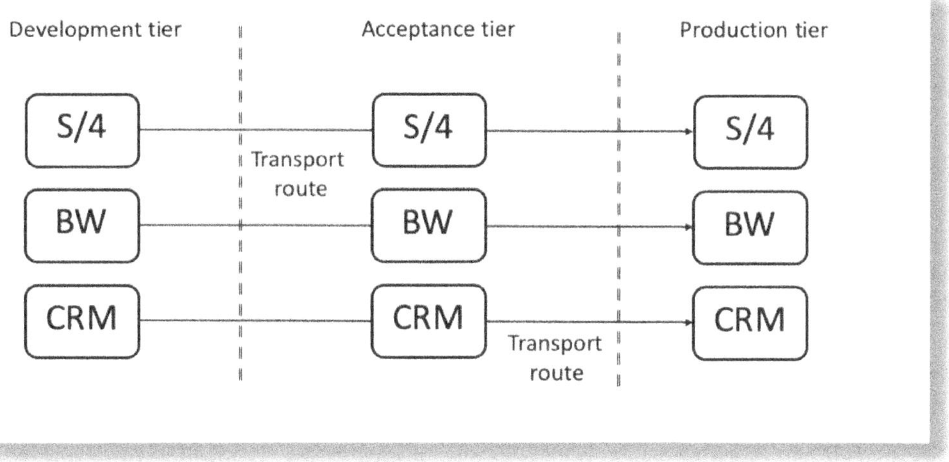

Figure 3.4: Development, acceptance and production tiers

3.5 Stack deployment

The disadvantage of the hybrid setup is the difference in the underlying technology between the systems installed on-premise and the systems in the Cloud. The on-premise SAP systems can be installed bare-metal or virtualized, using VMware. On Azure, they run on a customized version of Hyper-V. From an SAP perspective, running SAP heterogeneously is no issue. Running the development and acceptance systems on Windows and production system on Unix is also supported. We have seen installations in which, for the same system, some application servers were installed on Unix, while others were installed on Windows. Although it is technically possible, it is not recommended from a system administrative point of view because it unnecessarily complicates system management. In addition, most customers run both SAP and non-SAP applications, which complicates things even more. Running your IT infrastructure on a homogeneous environment is therefore strongly recommended.

This is where Azure Stack comes in. Azure Stack extends Azure capabilities to an on-premise installation and allows you to install an Azure Cloud in your data center.

Azure Stack has the following advantages:

- The Azure services and capabilities can be extended to on-premise systems. In most installations, non-production systems are installed in the Cloud, while production systems remain on-premise. Azure Stack enables you to deploy applications consistently, both cloud and non-cloud.
- You can streamline your setup between cloud and non-cloud, including off-site backup, site recovery, cloud-based monitoring, and much more.

Azure Stack HCI (Hyper Converged Infrastructure) is an extension of Azure Stack (see Figure 3.5). It is sold as an integrated system of software and validated hardware. It ensures the underlying compatibility between the underlying cloud and non-cloud infrastructure.

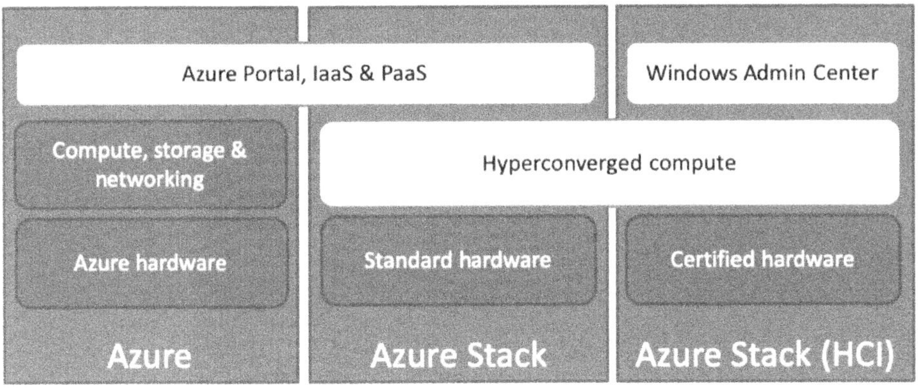

Figure 3.5: Azure Stack layout

The hardware arrives pre-installed and pre-configured. It is purpose-built, allowing you to get up and running quickly. The Azure Stack HCI systems are available from Hewlett Packard Enterprise, Dell EMC, Cisco, Lenovo, and many other suppliers. Azure Stack HCI can be used to combine the public cloud with a private cloud, or it can be disconnected from the public cloud, using it as a private cloud deployed in your own data center or at a service provider.

4 High availability and disaster recovery

High availability and disaster recovery are like insurance policies. You need to be prepared for "what if" scenarios. As with any insurance policy, you need to balance the cost against the event you want to protect yourself from. The more coverage you have, the more protected you are; and the more expensive the policy becomes.

4.1 High availability

High availability means that when there's a problem with the primary system, a secondary system can immediately take over, with little down time and no loss of data. In most cases, this is an automated process. You require clustering software and shared storage in order to do this. Because data is shared between the cluster nodes, the clustering software can easily handle failover and fallback.

The difference between high availability and disaster recovery is that the former is used to protect the application and database from a hardware failure, whereas the latter is used to protect against a disaster at data-center level. High availability restarts the application as fast as possible on the secondary node, whereas disaster recovery recovers and restarts all applications in a secondary data center. For disaster recovery, concepts such as Recovery Point Objective (RPO) and Recovery Time Objective (RTO) come into play.

- A *Recovery Point Objective* (RPO) is the maximum period of time from which data may be lost due to a major incident. The RPO gives systems designers a maximum target time to work within. For instance, if the RPO is set to four hours, the aim is to lose no more than four hours of data. In practice, a daily off-site backup on tape will not suffice. Solutions such as database mirroring or data replication need to be considered.

- A *Recovery Time Objective* (RTO) is the targeted duration of time within which a system must be available again after a failure occurs. The aim is to avoid unacceptable consequences. For example, if the RTO is set to four hours, then, in practice, the production system must be up and running within four hours of the interruption starting.

Traditionally, high availability and disaster recovery result in large standby systems sitting idle for most of their lives. Businesses with high requirements go one step further and operate a remote data center to which they can failover if the worst of the worst should happen.

4.2 Disaster recovery

Disaster recovery is a methodology which consists of a set of procedures and best practices to enable the recovery or continuation of the data center, systems, databases and applications, following a disaster. There are two types of disasters, natural and man-made. The first category includes natural disasters such as floods, hurricanes, tornadoes and earthquakes. The second category includes man-made disasters such as infrastructure failure, failed implementation projects and general human errors. Protecting against a natural disaster is complicated, but possible. Many areas are well-known for floods, tornadoes or earthquakes. Building your data center next to a volcano would not be a good idea. For man-made disasters, change management is a must-have. Disaster recovery focuses on the systems and applications supporting critical business functions.

Prior to selecting a disaster-recovery strategy, a business continuity plan should be set up. The business continuity plan should indicate the RPO and RTO for various business processes (e.g., processes to run payroll, generate an order, etc.). These numbers, specified by business processes, are then mapped to the underlying applications, databases and systems supporting those processes.

Setting up disaster recovery procedures is not only a technical endeavor. It is up to management and key business users to define the RPO and RTO. Once these are clearly defined, technical solutions have to be implemented to match these requirements.

You also need to consider high availability and disaster recovery in the Cloud. Remember that an IaaS cloud provider basically provides you with compute, storage and network resources. It is up to you to configure them as needed. Thanks to the capacity, agility and elasticity discussed earlier, you can configure a minimal standby environment to which data is synchronized. The standby environment only needs to be increased to full capacity when required; i.e., during disaster recovery—either a rehearsal or a real failover. This has a positive impact on the cost of maintaining a fallback environment. In addition, many cloud providers have data centers all over the globe, which is difficult for non-IT companies to achieve.

4.3 SAP components

The first step in implementing high availability is the identification of the single points of failure (SPOFs) from an SAP NetWeaver Application Server perspective (see Figure 4.1).

An SAP system consists of the following components:

- Central Services Instance (SCS)—note that in order to distinguish between ABAP and Java based systems, the ABAP Central Services Instance is called A(SCS).
- at least one SAP Application Server, preferably two
- Enqueue Replication Server (ERS)
- the database, which can be AnyDB (DB2, Oracle, MaxDB, SQL Server or Sybase) or SAP HANA.

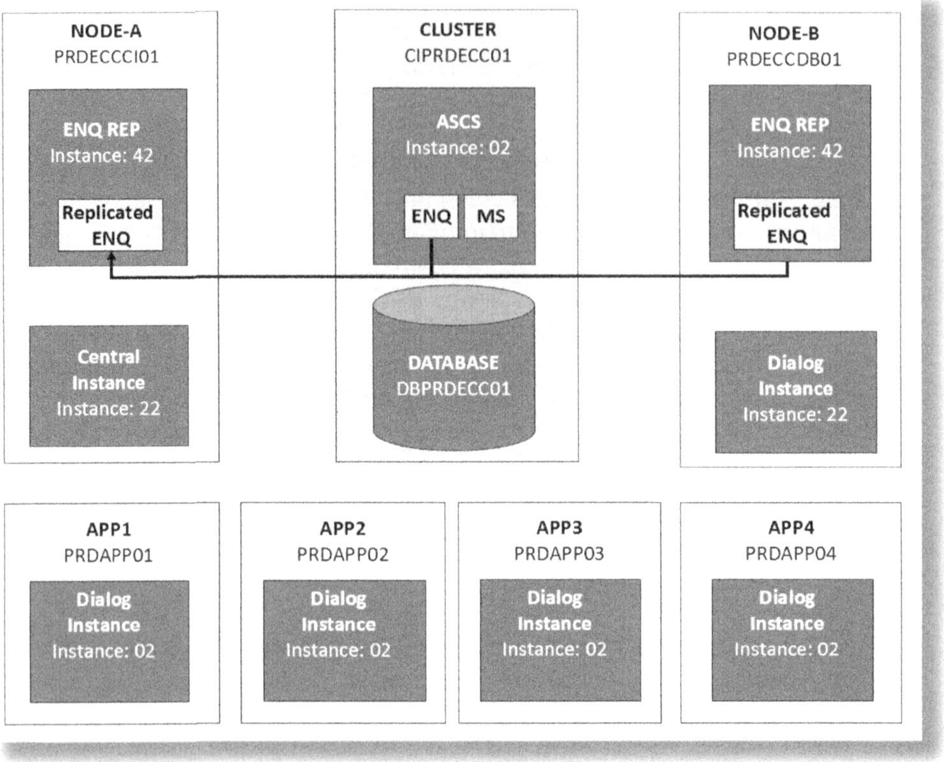

Figure 4.1: Identifying the single points of failure (SPOFs)

4.3.1 SAP Central Services

The SAP Central Services Instance comprises the message server and enqueue server. For ABAP-based systems, it is called ABAP SAP Central Services A(SCS). For Java-based systems it is just called SAP Central Services (SCS).

SAP Message Server

The message server is used to exchange and regulate messages between SAP instances and application servers. It is responsible for balancing the user load and is not too critical. When it fails, it needs to be restarted as soon as possible because users will be unable to log on; however, users already connected will not be impacted. When it is restarted, it queries all application servers for their status and performance statistics, and load balancing can resume as it did before.

SAP Enqueue Server

The enqueue server manages the locking of business objects at the SAP transaction level. Locks are set in a lock table, which is stored in the shared memory of the host on which the enqueue server runs. Failure of this service has a significant effect on the system because all transactions that contain locks must be rolled back, and any SAP updates being processed fail.

4.3.2 The Primary Application Server

Today, the Primary Application Server (PAS) is an application server just like any other. In older SAP releases, this was called the Central Instance and included the Central Services, message server and enqueue server. The only difference between PAS and the other application servers is that the PAS is still the location where an SAP upgrade is done.

4.3.3 Additional application servers

Depending on the size of the SAP system, the transaction load and the number of concurrent users, the primary application server might not be enough. As such, additional application servers might need to be installed.

4.3.4 Enqueue Replication Server

The Enqueue Replication Server (ERS) runs on a host, separate to the Central Services Instance, and contains a replica of the lock table. If the SCS instance with the enqueue server fails, it must be restarted on the host on which the ERS is running. The restarted enqueue server copies the lock table from the ERS to generate the new lock table.

4.3.5 The database

All customization and business data reside in the database. As such, the database is the most important component in the SAP system landscape. Many SAP system administrators and consultants do not realize that SAP Application Servers consist of the SAP kernel and several configuration files. The SAP kernel can be compared to an interpreter. It reads ABAP or Java code from within the database and executes it on the platform it runs. If one of my customers called me today saying that all was lost except for the last database backup, I would tell them not to worry—we would be able to recover it.

Table 4.1 summarizes the mandatory components that make up an SAP system, highlighting the database and SCS instance as single points of failure.

Component	Number of components in an SAP system	Single point of failure
SCS instance (message server and enqueue server)	1	YES
Database instance	1	YES
Primary Application Server (PAS)	1	No (if you install at least one additional application server)
Additional application servers	X	No (if you install more than one)
Enqueue Replication Server (ERS)	At least two	No

Table 4.1: Mandatory SAP components and SPOFs

4.4 In the Cloud

In the end, everything is built on hardware, cloud or no cloud. Even in the Cloud, hardware can, and will, fail. In the Azure Cloud, you select a region in which you want to deploy your virtual machines; no more, no less. You cannot choose which physical machine your virtual machine will be deployed on; and physical machines, no matter how resilient, can fail.

There are three scenarios that can impact the availability of a virtual machine in Azure:

- Unexpected downtime due to a hardware, rack, storage or network failure—when this happens, the virtual machines are migrated to, and restarted on, another physical machine. Your system is unavailable during migration and restart.
- Unplanned hardware maintenance—if the Azure platform receives too many errors from a physical machine, thereby indicating future failure, then any virtual machines on it are migrated to a healthy physical machine. The migration is done online using Live Migration. The operation only pauses the virtual machines for a short time. Memory, open files, and network connections are maintained, but performance might be reduced during the operation.
- Planned maintenance events—these are periodic updates made by Microsoft to improve reliability, performance and security of the underlying infrastructure. Most of these updates are done without impacting the virtual machines; however, there are rare cases in which in an update is needed, requiring a reboot of your virtual machine.

Fortunately, opportunities exist to ensure system availability and to provide protection against the previously-mentioned unplanned downtimes. However, it is your decision, and your responsibility, whether to implement them or not.

4.4.1 Affinity groups

Affinity groups can be used to ensure that your systems remain close together in the data center in order to guarantee optimal performance. When you create an affinity group, Azure keeps the systems as physically close to each other as possible.

This used to be very important because huge amounts of data are transferred between SAP systems. For example, a significant amount of the master data from the SAP CRM system resides in the SAP ERP system. Many transactions in the SAP CRM system perform remote function calls to SAP ERP.

Due to the significant performance improvements in the Azure data centers, it is no longer necessary to define affinity groups.

Proximity placement groups

Microsoft recently introduced proximity placement groups. This is a new logical grouping capability for your virtual machines that are deployed on Azure. When you deploy VMs in Azure, you can select a region, not a data center. A region consists of several data centers. This means that your VMs might be distributed among several data centers. When you assign your VMs to the same proximity placement group, they are placed in the same data center. This improves performance and reduces network latency. This is a very important feature because huge amounts of data are transferred between the different SAP components (SAP SCS, SAP Application Server, database). It can also have a positive impact on communication between SAP systems, such as SAP ERP and CRM. For more information see *https://azure.microsoft.com/en-us/blog/introducing-proximity-placement-groups*.

4.4.2 Availability sets

You can use availability sets to group systems. Systems in an availability set are isolated from each other when deployed within the data center.

Each virtual machine in an availability set is assigned to an update domain and a fault domain. Update and fault domains have a significant impact on the availability of a virtual machine:

- Virtual machines in the same update domain might be automatically updated by Microsoft (see Figure 4.2). An availability set is assigned to five update domains by default. This can be increased to 20 update domains. When more than five virtual machines are configured within a single availability set, the sixth virtual machine is placed into the same update domain as the first virtual machine; the seventh is placed in the same update domain as the second virtual machine, and so on. This implies that when you put ten virtual machines in the same availability set, two are impacted during planned maintenance. The update domains might not be rebooted sequentially during maintenance, and only one update domain is rebooted at a time.
- Virtual machines in the same fault domain share a common power source and physical network switch. By default, the virtual machines configured in an availability set are separated by up to two fault domains. The maximum number of fault domains is three.

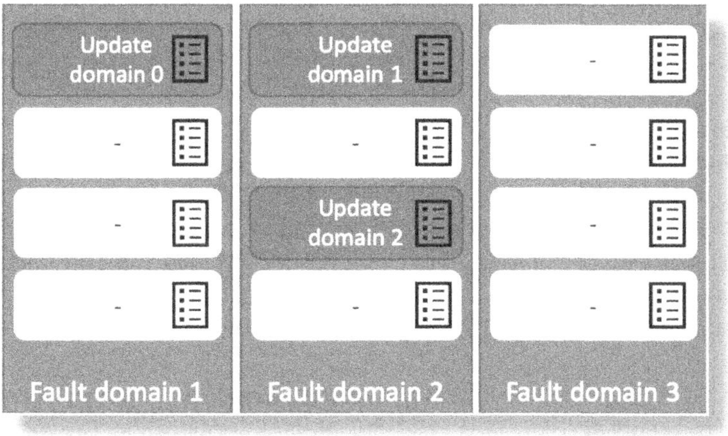

Figure 4.2: Hardware layout in Azure

While placing your virtual machines into an availability set does not protect your application from operating system failures or application-specific failures, it does limit the impact of planned maintenance, potential physical hardware failures, network outages, and power interruptions.

An availability set ensures that:

- all virtual machines are part of the same update domain. An update domain, for example, makes sure that the virtual machines aren't updated at the same time during planned maintenance downtime.
- all virtual machines are part of the same fault domain. A fault domain, for example, makes sure that virtual machines are deployed so that no single point of failure affects the availability of all virtual machines.

How can availability sets be used in the context of SAP systems?

SAP Central Services

Use a separate availability set for the Central Services Instance, consisting of two virtual machines (see Figure 4.3)—one for the SCS and another for the ERS. Deploying Windows Failover Cluster (Windows) or Pacemaker (Linux) combined with the Azure Load Balancer ensures a 99.95% availability of the Central Services Instance.

The Central Services Instance is a single point of failure. It hosts two critical components: the message server and more importantly, the enqueue server. The ERS maintains a copy of the enqueue table in memory on the secondary VM. To optimize availability, you should install two identical virtual machines containing both a Central Services Instance and an Enqueue Replication Server. In this setup, the SCS is active on the primary VM, while an ERS service is active on the secondary VM. Locking information is constantly synchronized between the primary and the secondary VMs via the ERS service. When the primary VM fails, the Windows Failover Cluster activates the SCS service on the secondary VM. The SCS service reads the locking table from the ERS service to get the latest version.

The SCS service also hosts the global directory which contains crucial configuration and log files used by all SAP Application Servers. This directory is shared between all nodes in an on-premise cluster layout. Azure does not offer this functionality. Instead, you can use SIOS DataKeeper, a third-party software, to create a mirrored storage that simulates shared storage. Another alternative is to use a file share to deploy the SAP global files. The fileserver on which the file share resides must not be a single point of failure. This can be achieved by using a Scale-Out File Server Cluster (Windows), Azure NetApp Files for SAP Applications (SUSE), or GlusterFS (Red Hat).

Finally, an Azure Load Balancer is needed between both the virtual machines, and avoids unexpected downtime. The Load Balancer ensures that during downtime, incoming requests are directed to the failover instance.

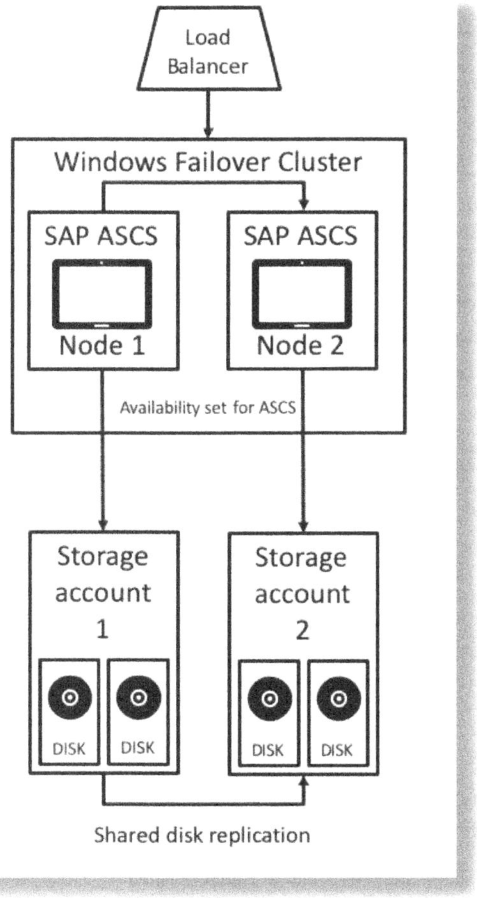

Figure 4.3: High availability layout for the (A)SCS instance

Using Autostart for the Central Services Instance

An alternative option is to use SAP's Autostart functionality. When there is an unplanned downtime in the infrastructure, the VM of the SCS is restarted on another available server. Azure only restarts the VM and not the application installed within. To ensure that the SCS instance starts automatically after the VM reboots, you need to set the Autostart parameter. This setup is much easier to configure and maintain than using an availability set. However, it implies that in the case of a hardware failure, although it may be short, SAP will possibly be unavailable.

SAP Application Servers

Use availability sets for the SAP Application Servers. To provide redundancy, group two or more virtual machines in one availability set. This ensures that during a planned maintenance, at least one of the virtual machines remains available to meet the 99.95% Azure SLA. This also ensures that the virtual machines do not reside on the same physical machine, and so cannot be impacted by unplanned hardware maintenance or downtime. An Azure Load Balancer is not needed because SAP uses the load balancing functionality of the message server which resides in the Central Services Instance.

If a node in Azure fails, all virtual machines are automatically restarted on another node. If Autostart is configured for the SAP Application Server, it is started automatically and re-connected to the message server, which considers it available again.

Autostart for SAP Application Servers

By default, SAP does not automatically start when the operating system does; but the functionality to do so exists. Setting parameter Autostart=1 in the instance profile does the trick. However, SAP does not recommend this because there is no control in the order of instance restarts when multiple VMs, or one VM with multiple SAP instances inside, restart. There is normally a one-to-one relationship in Azure (one application server = one VM). The possibility of more than one restarting at the same time is almost non-existent thanks to availability sets. As such, the Autostart can be enabled.

Web Dispatcher

The SAP Web Dispatcher is a software solution which sits between your SAP system and the Internet. The Web Dispatcher is a software firewall and proxy, and is the entry point for HTTP(s) requests to your SAP system. It behaves like a load balancer and evenly distributes load between the different SAP instances. The SAP Web Dispatcher supports many communication scenarios such as HTTP(s), SSL Termination, SSL re-encryption, and X.509 client certificate authentication. If SAP Web Dispatcher is used in internet-facing scenarios (e.g., mobile applications), it becomes a single point of failure. You should install at least two Web Dispatchers and include them in an Azure availability set. Azure Load Balancer is needed to distribute the load between both Web Dispatchers and to intercept unexpected downtime. Autostart can be used to restart the Web Dispatcher after failover.

The database

All customization and business data reside in the database. As such, the database is the most important component in the SAP system landscape. Protecting the database is comparable to on-premise solutions. It is based on the database technology itself and has little to do with Azure. For SQL Server, you can choose between log shipping, database mirroring, or always on. For Sybase, you have to use Sybase Replication Server.

The only thing that you need to do is to include the primary and standby database instances in the same availability set, and set up Azure Load Balancer between the two instances. Apart from that, the deployment and configuration is the same as for on-premise.

Storage accounts are SPOFs!

Don't forget that an Azure storage account is a single point of failure. It is therefore important to have at least two storage accounts in which your virtual machines are equally distributed. This is not the case with managed disks. Managed disks are automatically aligned with the availability set of the virtual machine they are attached to. Disks in the availability set are isolated from each other to avoid a single point of failure. If the storage fails, only the VM with attached disks fails. As with availability sets for virtual machines, the others are not impacted.

Finally, virtual machines can also experience downtime in the unlikely event of an outage or a disaster that affects an entire data center, or an entire region. For these scenarios, Azure provides protection options such as availability zones and paired regions. If one zone or data center is compromised, the replicated applications and data are instantly available in another predefined zone.

4.4.3 Availability zones

An availability zone is a physically separate location within an Azure Region. Every region has a minimum of three separate zones. Each availability zone is made up of one or more data centers equipped with independent power, cooling, and networking. Availability zones enable customers to run mission-critical applications with high availability and low-latency replication.

Many large and medium-sized companies operate their SAP applications from two data centers that are within close proximity. In this setup, half of the productive SAP landscape is installed in the primary data center and the other half is installed in the secondary data center (see Figure 4.4). The SAP Application Servers are divided among both data centers. A Failover Cluster is used to protect the SAP Central Services Instance and database. Database availability can be enhanced by using database replication or mirroring. Load balancers are needed to guide end users to the active SAP Central Services Instance and database.

Companies with greater high-availability and disaster-recovery requirements take this setup one step further and operate a third data center. This minimizes the impact of natural disasters such as hurricanes and floods, and man-made disasters such as grid failures or political unrest. The systems in the third data center are, in most cases, inactive or in standby mode. The infrastructure is installed and configured, and applications are deployed ready to be started up when needed. Data is synchronized between the primary, secondary and standby databases, with database or storage replication.

An availability zone within Azure is the Cloud alternative to a remote data center. The advantage is that the data center is taken care of by the service provider. Installing and operating data centers is expensive. You need to consider power, electricity and dedicated network connections to and from the data center. In the Cloud you only pay for what you use.

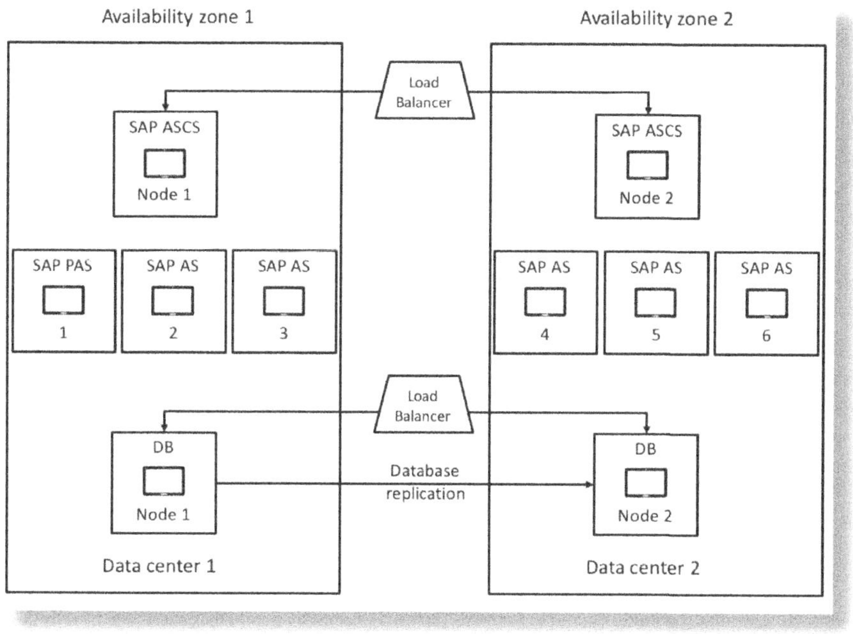

Figure 4.4: Increasing availability using zones

There is no additional cost for deploying virtual machines in availability zones. There is, however, an additional cost for data transfer between virtual machines residing in different zones.

4.5 Recommended design

Microsoft guarantees the following SLA's for virtual machines deployed in Azure (see Figure 4.5):

- For all virtual machines that have two or more instances deployed across two or more availability zones in the same Azure Region, Microsoft guarantees virtual machine connectivity to at least one instance at least 99.99% of the time.
- For all virtual machines that have two or more instances deployed in the same availability set, Microsoft guarantees virtual machine connectivity to at least one instance at least 99.95% of the time.
- For all single-instance virtual machines using premium storage for all operating system and data disks, Microsoft guarantees virtual machine connectivity at least 99.9% of the time.

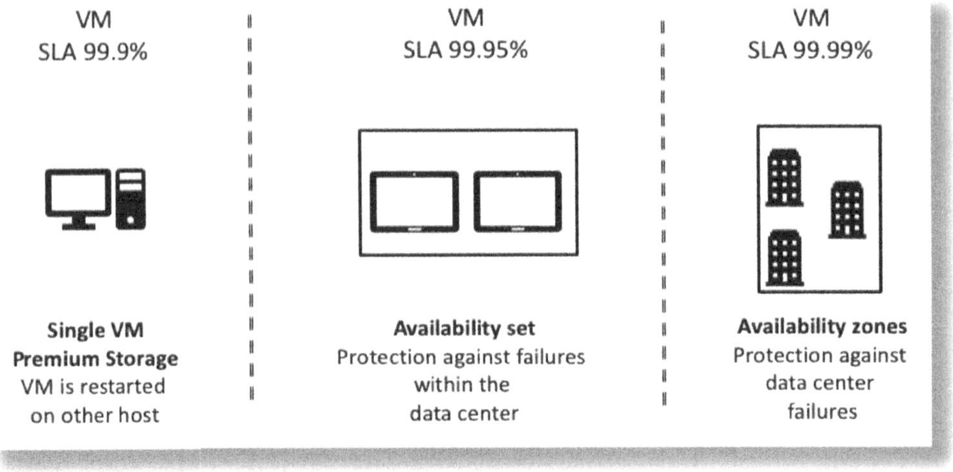

Figure 4.5: SLA on Azure

When designing a high-availability SAP landscape in Azure, you should take the following configuration considerations into account (see Figure 4.6):

- Your SAP landscape should be configured in a three-tier layout, meaning separation of the SAP Application Server layer from the RDBMS layer.
- In addition to the above point, the SCS instance should be separated from the PAS and should be installed on a dedicated virtual machine.
- The SCS must be duplicated on two virtual machines using the ERS. A Windows Failover Cluster (Windows), or Pacemaker (Linux), and a load balancer must be configured between both nodes. The SAP global folder needs to be duplicated between the two virtual machines using the SIOS DataKeeper replication. Both VM's need to be in the same availability set.
- You need at least two application servers on two virtual machines in a dedicated availability set. The Autostart parameter must be set to make sure that the application server restarts if the virtual machine restarts.
- You need to use database high-availability features; for example, SAP HANA System Replication, SQL Server AlwaysOn or Sybase Replication Server. The virtual machines running the database instances need to be in the same availability set.
- The SAP landscape needs to be within one virtual network.

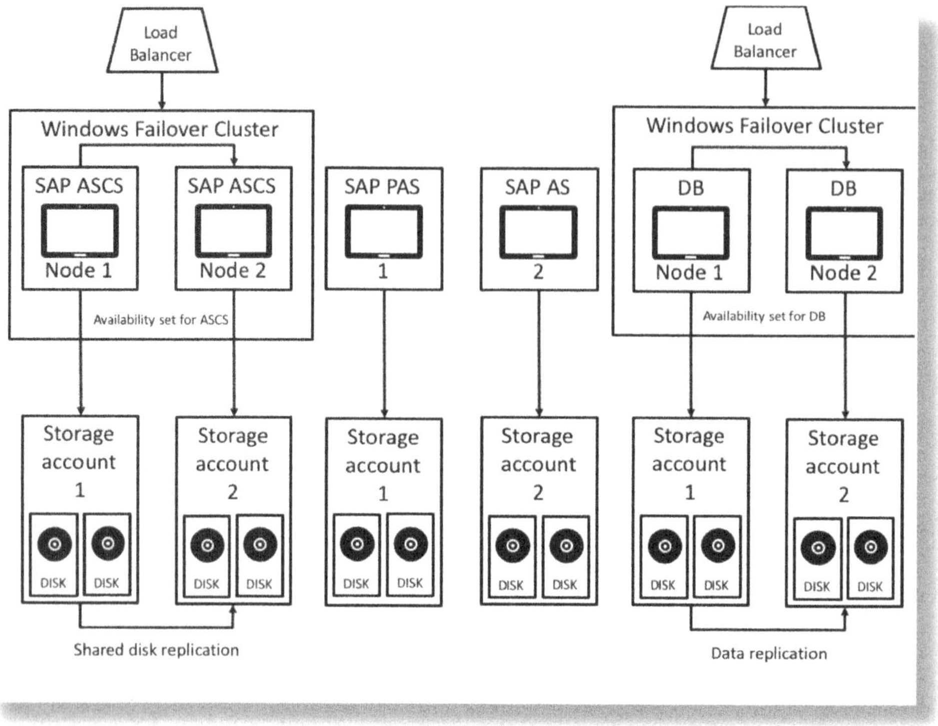

Figure 4.6: Recommended design for high availability

4.6 Backup and recovery

Data loss due to hardware failures is unlikely thanks to the many capabilities offered by Azure. Virtual machines can be protected by availability sets and zones. Storage is threefold in different locations. A backup might sound less important in such an environment; however, a proper backup and recovery strategy is still a must in order to overcome human errors.

Azure Backup is a service for backing up and restoring data in the Cloud. Many customers use this service to back up on-premise systems in the Cloud, thereby replacing off-site backup solutions. The advantage of cloud backup is like any solution in the Cloud—scalability and flexibility. You can extend it as needed and only pay for what you use.

Azure Backup has the following advantages over on-premise backup solutions:

- Automatic storage management and unlimited scaling—Azure Backup automatically allocates and manages storage in a pay-as-you-go model. This means that you never run out of space and that you only pay for what you consume.
- High availability—storage replication is integrated into the backup solution. There are two types of replication: locally redundant storage and geo-redundant storage. Locally redundant storage (LRS) maintains three copies of your data. All copies of the data exist

within the same Azure Region. Geo-redundant storage (GRS) is the default and is the recommended replication option. GRS replicates your data into a secondary Azure Region. GRS provides an elevated level of high availability, even if there is a regional outage.

- Data encryption—data is transferred and stored in an encrypted format.
- Database-consistent backups, or database-aware backups—these are recorded by the database.
- Long-term retention—Recovery Services vaults can be used for short-term and long-term data retention. You can keep up to 9999 recovery points per protected instance. A *protected instance* is a virtual machine, application or database for which a backup policy exists.

Azure Backup consists of different components or agents that need to be deployed on the servers you want to protect. All data is saved to a Recovery Services vault.

What is a Recovery Services vault?

A vault is a room (for example, in a bank) with thick walls and a strong door, used to store money or valuable items in safe conditions. A Recovery Services vault is exactly the same thing, but for crucial business data. You can use vaults to hold backup data from applications, databases, operating systems and servers, whether deployed in the Cloud or on-premise. Backups are saved on backup storage. Azure Backup uses block blob storage to back up your instances. You have the flexibility to choose between locally redundant storage (LRS) or geo-redundant storage (GRS). Both LRS and GRS are block blob storage.

How does Azure Backup work?

In order to back up on-premise systems to the Azure Cloud:

- The backup can be done directly to Azure by using the Microsoft Azure Recovery Services (MARS). Note that Linux and Unix systems are not supported by MARS.

- The backup can also be done via a backup server—either System Center Data Protection Manager (DPM) or Microsoft Azure Backup Server (MABS). In this scenario, machines and workloads back up to MABS/DPM. Then, in a second step, MABS/DPM backs up to a vault in Azure using the MARS agent.

To back up systems in the Azure Cloud:

- You can back up specific files and folders on the Azure VM by running the MARS agent inside the VM.
- You can back up the VM directly using the Azure VM Backup Extension. This extension backs up the entire VM using snapshot technology. These backups are also known as recovery points. The restore capability is not limited to the restore of the complete virtual machine. Specific files and folders can also be restored from within the virtual machines (see Figure 4.7). You only need to select the snapshot or recovery point from which you want to restore the missing file. Azure Recovery mounts the source disks, or file systems, to the original VM, or to any VM you choose. The missing file can then be easily retrieved from the mounted disk or file system. The Azure VM backup extension can be used to perform database-aware backups.

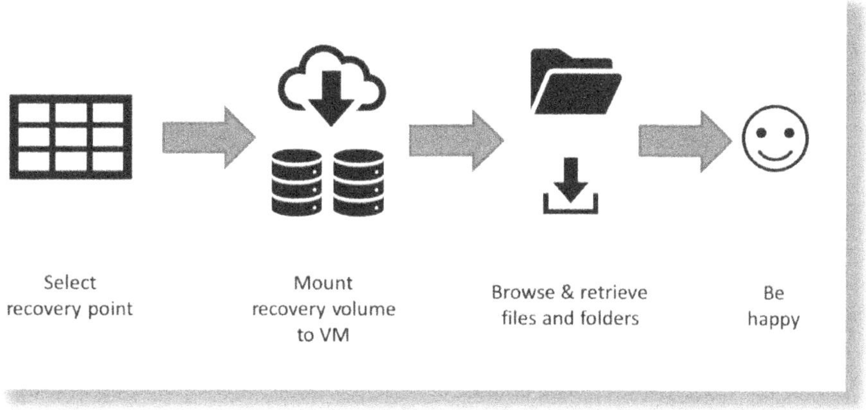

Figure 4.7: Using file restore from Azure Backup

Database-aware and database-unaware snapshots

A *database-aware snapshot* is a storage snapshot which, when taken, notifies the database. When the database is warned, it can save a consistent state to disk. Database-aware snapshots are therefore preferred over database-unaware snapshots. A *database-unaware snapshot* is a storage snapshot taken without notifying the database. When a recovery to the snapshot is done and the database is restarted, the database assumes that a power failure occurred and performs an online recovery. Database-unaware snapshots are, by definition, inconsistent, because the snapshot was taken while the database was running.

The different backup options and tools are listed in Table 4.2.

Component	Benefits	Limits	What is protected?	Where are backups stored?
Azure Backup (MARS) agent	Back up files and folders on physical or virtual Windows OS (Hyper-V and Azure). Can run without a backup server.	Not application-aware; file, folder, and volume-level restore only. No support for Linux.	Files, folders, and system state.	Recovery Services vault.
System Center DPM	Application-aware snapshots (VSS). Full flexibility for when to take backups. Recovery granularity (all). Can use Recovery Services vault. Linux support on Hyper-V and VMware VMs. Backup and restore VMware VMs.	Oracle not supported.	Files, folders, volumes, VMs, applications, workloads, and system state.	Recovery Services vault. Locally attached disk. Tape (on-premise only).

Compo-nent	Benefits	Limits	What is protected?	Where are backups stored?
Azure Backup Server	Application-aware snapshots (VSS). Full flexibility for when to take backups. Recovery granularity (all). Can use Recovery Services vault. Linux support on Hyper-V and VMware VMs. Backup and restore VMware VMs. Does not require a System Center license.	Oracle not sup-ported. Always requires live Azure sub-scription. No support for tape backup.	Files, folders, volumes, VMs, applications, workloads, and system state.	Recovery Services vault. Locally attached disk.
Azure VM Backup Extension	Application-aware snapshots (VSS). Native backups for Windows/ Linux. No specific agent installation required. Fabric-level backup with no backup infrastructure needed.	Back up VMs once a day. Restore VMs only at disk level. Cannot back up on-premise.	VMs and disks	Recovery Services vault.

Table 4.2: Azure backup options and tools

Recommendations for SAP

The Azure VM Backup extension can be used to back up a complete VM in Azure. This is the recommended solution for SAP Application Servers. SAP Application Servers are static; there is no business or data inside. Therefore, a full restore of the VM is acceptable.

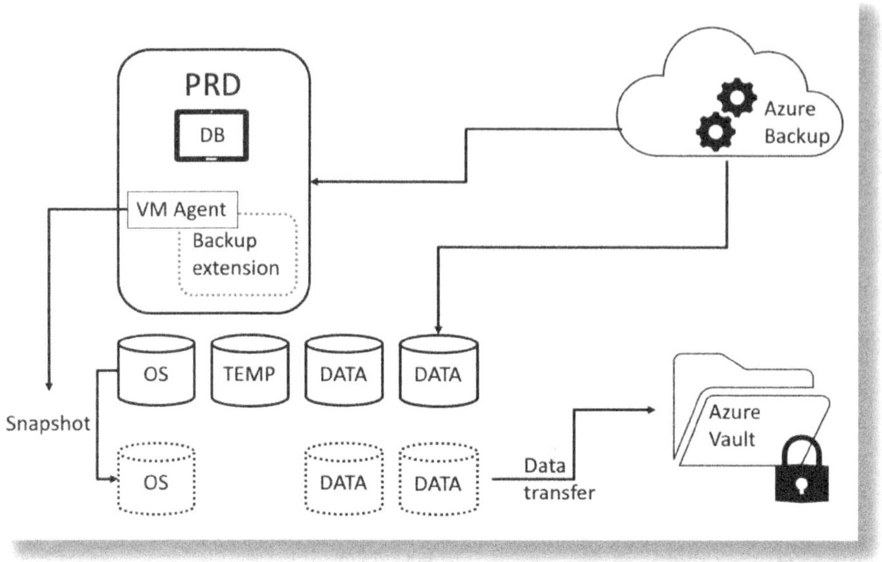

Figure 4.8: Azure Backup layout

You can also use the Azure VM Backup extension to take a database-consistent VM backup of Oracle and SQL Server databases using the Windows Volume Shadow Copy Service (VSS) (see Figure 4.8). At this time, there is no direct integration with IBM DB2, MaxDB, SAP ASE, and SAP HANA. For these databases you need to use a two-step approach to copy your backup to an Azure blob. First, you back up your database to disk using database technology. Then, you write the dump to blob storage; optionally, to a different region. Another option is to back up the database to a disk in a separate machine, and then back up that virtual machine using the Azure VM Backup extension.

Using Windows Volume Shadow Copy Service (VSS)

Backups using the VSS framework cannot be used for a point-in-time restore. Therefore, the recommendation is to perform database backups with RDBMS functionality instead of relying on the Azure VM Backup extension.

VSS does not exist on Linux

Windows has the VSS framework to ensure database-consistent VM backup, but there is no such generic framework for Linux. There is, however, a VSS-like framework to ensure application-consistent backups. This framework is available for all Linux distributions supported on Azure. It allows you to create prescripts and postscripts as part of the backup. These scripts can then be used to quiesce I/O while taking the snapshot. These scripts can be used with Oracle, SAP ASE and SAP HANA.

Backup using third-party tools

In addition to backing up your SAP environment using Azure Backup, you can also back up and recover your SAP environment using a third-party tool. The initial goal of most of these tools was to safeguard on-premise applications, databases, and systems (see Table 4.3). The configuration and administration of these tools is comparable to their on-premise counterparts.

Vendor	Product	Azure Marketplace	Integration with:
DELL EMC	Avamar Virtual Edition	Yes	DB2 Oracle native or via Backint SQL Server SAP ASE
DELL EMC	Networker Virtual Edition	Yes	DB2 Oracle native or via Backint SAP ASE SAP HANA SAP IQ SQL Server
Veritas	NetBackup	Yes	DB2 MaxDB Oracle native or via Backint SAP ASE SAP HANA SQL Server

Vendor	Product	Azure Marketplace	Integration with:
HPE	Data Protector	No	DB2 MaxDB Oracle native or via Backint SAP ASE SAP HANA SQL Server
IBM	Spectrum Protect (Tivoli)	No	DB2 Oracle SAP HANA SQL Server
CommVault		No	DB2 MaxDB Oracle native or via Backint SAP ASE SAP HANA SQL Server

Table 4.3: Third-party backup tools

What is Azure Marketplace?

Azure Marketplace is a rich catalog of thousands of products and end-to-end solutions from independent software vendors (ISVs). These software products are fully integrated with, and optimized for, Azure, and can be deployed within minutes. Most of them can even be licensed in a pay-as-you-go model.

5 Implementation guidelines

In this chapter, we list the implementation guidelines for the operating systems and databases supported in Azure. To get you started, we give an overview only, because Microsoft provides detailed documentation which is constantly being updated as new technology becomes available.

5.1 Operating systems

The following operating systems are available on Microsoft Azure and are supported by SAP:

- Microsoft Windows Server 2008 R2, 2012 (R2), 2016 and 2019
- SUSE Linux Enterprise Server (SLES) 12 and higher
- SUSE SLES for SAP Applications (based on SLES 12) and higher
- Red Hat Enterprise Linux (RHEL) 7 and higher
- Red Hat RHEL for SAP (based on RHEL 7) and higher

- Red Hat RHEL for SAP HANA (based on RHEL 7) and higher
- Oracle Linux 7

All SAP components running on NetWeaver 7.0 and higher are supported on Azure. The SAP kernel should be at 7.21 EXT build 622. If not, an SAP kernel upgrade is, in most cases, not an issue.

5.1.1 Using Windows

NetWeaver (as of version 7.0) is supported on Azure. In addition, the following products are also supported on Windows in Azure:

- SAP Business Objects Planning and Consolidation on NetWeaver
- SAP Business Objects BI Platform
- SAP Business Objects Data Services 4.2
- TREX 7.10
- SAP Content Server (at least version 6.50 and MaxDB 7.9)
- SAP Financial Consolidation 1.0 (at least SP06 and higher)

The SAP solutions listed above are supported on Azure in combination with:

- SQL Server, as of 2008 R2
- Sybase ASE, as of 16.0 SP02
- IBM DB2 for Linux
- Windows, as of 10.6
- Oracle, as of 11.2.0,
- MaxDB
- Live Cache, as of version 7.9

There are some prerequisites when operating SAP systems virtually, and these apply to Azure as well. If you operate a system on physical hardware, all existing resources are available for the operating system. If you operate a system on a virtual machine, the hypervisor sits between the virtual machine and the actual hardware resources. As hardware resources might be divided among several guest operating systems at the same time, important information about native resources available to the virtual system is missing.

To ensure SAP support in a virtual environment and in a cloud environment on Windows, it is mandatory to set up enhanced SAP System Monitoring, as described in SAP Note 1409604—"Virtualization on Windows: Enhanced monitoring". It basically comes down to setting up SAP tools for data collection, making sure that you run the latest version of the SAP Host Agent, and installing some SAP notes to enable monitoring from within the ABAP system. On the virtual machine, the VM agent must be installed. This is done by default. In addition, Windows Azure PowerShell and the PowerShell cmdlets created for Azure Enhanced Monitoring should be deployed.

5.1.2 Using Linux

In addition to NetWeaver, the following products are also supported on Linux in Azure:

- SAP Business Objects BI Platform
- SAP Business Objects Data Services 4.2
- TREX 7.10 on SLES or RHEL
- SAP Content Server (minimum version 6.50 and MaxDB 7.9)

These SAP solutions are supported on Azure in combination with:

- Sybase ASE, as of 16.0 SP02
- IBM DB2 for Linux
- Windows, as of 10.6,
- Oracle, as of 11.2.04,
- MaxDB
- Live Cache, as of version 7.9.

SAP HANA is supported with SLES and RHEL on virtual machines as listed in the SAP HANA Hardware Directory.

On Windows, there are some prerequisites for obtaining support from SAP; this is the same as when operating SAP systems virtually. It is mandatory to set up the enhanced SAP System Monitoring, as described in SAP Note 2191498—"SAP on Linux with Azure: Enhanced Monitoring". This involves setting up SAP tools for data collection, making sure that you run the latest version of the SAP Host Agent and installing some SAP notes to enable monitoring from within the ABAP system. On the virtual machine, the VM agent must be installed. By default, the SAP system can only see the resources assigned to the virtual machine. The actual hardware resources are hidden. These tools allow the SAP system to see beyond the hypervisor and get information about the native hardware resources which would otherwise be missing.

5.2 Databases

SAP is available for many different hardware platforms and database systems. All this is changing in 2025, when SAP components will only be supported on SAP HANA. For the time being, SAP is still supported on IBM DB2, MaxDB, Oracle, SAP HANA, SQL Server and Sybase.

5.2.1 Using IBM DB2

SAP on IBM DB2 for LUW on Azure is supported as of DB2 version 10.5 on Windows, SUSE Enterprise Linux and Red Hat Linux. When running SAP on DB2 on Azure, all system administration and development tools used on-premise can be used as they are.

There are some differences between running DB2 virtually or on bare metal:

- Storage recommendations do not differ between bare metal and virtual. Deploying the database on managed disks is strongly recommended. As with all databases, using network drives or shares to deploy the database data and log files is not supported. To increase performance, consider using Windows Storage Pools or Logical Volume Management (Linux).

- The backup/restore functionality supported on standard Windows or Linux installations is equally supported in the Cloud. Note, however, that DB2 on Windows does not support the Windows VSS technology. As a result, the application-consistent VM backup cannot be used for VMs used for the DB2 database.
- DB2 high availability and disaster recovery (HADR) is supported. If the virtual machines of the high-availability configuration have working-name resolution, the setup in Azure does not differ from any setup that is done on-premise.
- Microsoft Cluster Server (MSCS) is not supported.

For more information, see SAP Note 2233094—"DB6: SAP Applications on Azure Using IBM DB2 for Linux, UNIX, and Windows - Additional Information".

For information about supported SAP products and Azure VM types, refer to SAP Note 1928533—"SAP Applications on Azure: Supported Products and Azure VM types".

5.2.2 Using MaxDB

MaxDB is an SAP proprietary database. It started in 1977 as a research project. In the early 1980s, it became ADABAS. In 1997, SAP acquired the software from Software AG and developed it as SAP DB. In 2003, it was re-branded as MaxDB.

SAP currently supports MaxDB for use with all NetWeaver-based products, with SAP Content Server and liveCache. SAP liveCache is the in-memory version of MaxDB. It is used in combination with SAP Supply Chain Management (SCM) and SAP Extended Warehouse Management (EWM) solutions.

The SAP requirements for running SAP on MaxDB on Azure are:

- The minimum version should be 7.9. The same applies for the ODBC and JDBC drivers.

- Storage recommendations do not differ between bare metal and virtual. The MaxDB data volumes should be installed on a drive other than the MaxDB log volumes.
- If the number of IOPS per disk satisfies your requirements, all data volumes can be installed on the same disk, and the log volumes on another disk. If more IOPS are needed, it is recommended to use Windows Storage Pools or Linux Logical Volumes. This is much easier than manually dividing volumes among disks.
- Backing up and restoring a database in Azure works the same way as it does for on-premise systems. You can use standard SAP MaxDB backup/restore tools, which are described in the SAP MaxDB documentation documents listed in SAP Note 767598—"Available SAP MaxDB documentation". For performance reasons, you might consider using Windows Storage Pools or Linux Logical Volumes as you would for the data and log volumes.

SAP liveCache

In addition to the standard relational database, SAP SCM systems also require a second database—SAP liveCache. This is an in-memory database management system, which means that in normal operation all data is loaded into the main memory of the server (with persistent storage of the data on disk volumes). When data is loaded into SAP liveCache, its representation is also changed. Instead of the normal relational format, which would require complex traversals of many tables via key relations, an object-based representation is used. This is known as the Object Management Store (OMS). Only a small fraction of the data in SAP liveCache is stored in relational tables.

Technologically, SAP liveCache is built on the MaxDB database platform, with which it shares many architectural features (but not its memory-centric and object-based nature). SAP liveCache uses the same database administration tools as MaxDB.

You need to take the following into account when implementing SAP liveCache on Azure:

- Because SAP liveCache is an application that performs huge calculations, the amount and speed of RAM and CPU has a major influence on the SAP liveCache performance. It is therefore recommended to use the most recent D-series or M-series.

- SAP liveCache intensively uses computational power, so for productive usage it has to be deployed on a dedicated Azure virtual machine.
- SAP liveCache has the same database layout as MaxDB. The recommendation to separate data from database logs applies. As with all other RDBMS deployments, it is advisable to use Azure Premium Storage for performance-critical volumes.
- Backup and restore recommendations are the same as for MaxDB.

SAP Content Server

SAP Content Server is a stand-alone component in which a large quantity of electronic documents of any format, and with any content, can be stored. The documents can be saved either in one or more MaxDB instances, or in the file system. In this section, we discuss the SAP Content Server using the MaxDB option.

You should take the following into account when installing SAP Content Server on Azure:

- Only SAP Content Server 6.50 with MaxDB 7.9 or higher is supported.
- SAP Content Server is built on MaxDB technology. Therefore, all storage recommendations apply.
- Standard storage (HDD) might be considered for latency-insensitive applications (e.g., storing of invoices, contracts, etc.)

For more information on deploying MaxDB on Azure see: *https://docs.microsoft.com/en-us/azure/virtual-machines/workloads/sap/dbms_guide_maxdb*.

5.2.3 Using Oracle

As with the other databases, most recommendations for installing Oracle on bare metal also apply to installing Oracle virtually.

The following considerations should be taken into account:

- Oracle is only supported on Windows and Oracle Linux 7. Running the Oracle database on SLES and RHEL is not supported. SAP Application Servers use the Oracle Database Client and are therefore also not supported on SLES and RHEL. SAP Components which do not use the Oracle Database Client, such as the Central Services Instance, the Enqueue Replication Server or the Web Dispatcher, are supported on SLES and RHEL. However, it remains to be seen if running your SAP components on different operating systems is an advisable option. Technically, it is perfectly possible, but is not advisable from a system administration and support perspective.
- For backup and recovery, the SAP BR*Tools for Oracle are supported in the same way as for Windows running on bare metal. Oracle Recovery Manager (RMAN) is also supported to back up and restore, both to and from disk. You can also use Azure Backup to run an application-consistent VM backup. The Oracle releases supported on Azure can be used with the VSS functionality for backups. Detailed documentation on how to implement Oracle with VSS is available at: *https://docs.oracle.com/en/database/oracle/oracle-database/12.2/ntqrf/basic-concepts-of-database-backup-and-recovery-with-vss.html#GUID-E80A9CAC-A3BD-4C07-AD75-97FED36EB6C0*.
- Oracle Data Guard is supported and can be used in high-availability setups. For more information about disaster recovery for Oracle databases in Azure, see: *https://docs.microsoft.com/en-us/azure/virtual-machines/workloads/oracle/oracle-disaster-recovery*.

Storage recommendations

An Oracle database consists of several table spaces. Every table space has at least one data file. For performance reasons, these data files should be distributed among different file systems.

By default, the Oracle database, in combination with SAP, uses the file-system and tablespace layout defined in Table 5.1.

Name	Description	Disk	Caching	Storage Pool or Logical Volumes
/oracle/<SID>/origlogA	Original set A of redo logs	Premium	None	Can be used
/oracle/<SID>/origlogB	Original set B of redo logs	Premium	None	Can be used
/oracle/<SID>/mirrlogA	Mirrored set A of redo logs	Premium	None	Can be used
/oracle/<SID>/mirrlogB	Mirrored set B of redo logs	Premium	None	Can be used
/oracle/<SID>/oraarch	Archived log files	Premium	None	Not needed
/oracle/<SID>/sapdata 1	Data files for SYSTEM, TEMP, UNDO	Premium	None	Should be used
/oracle/<SID>/sapdata 2 .. x	Data-base for PSAPSR3	Premium	Read-only	Should be used

Table 5.1: Recommended filesystem layout for Oracle

Recommendations for the database layout are as follows:

- Using premium storage is strongly recommended. Using network drives and shares is not supported for performance and stability reasons.
- Storage Pools (Windows) or Logical Volumes (Linux) can be used to increase the number of IOPS and I/O performance. Storage Pools, or Logical Volumes, are large logical devices mounted on multiple disks. In addition to performance, they also simplify database administration and avoid the need to divide the datafiles across multiple disks.

- Normally, disk caching improves performance to read/write operations when a large amount of data is modified. However, read/write caching is not useful with Oracle because write I/O is done randomly. Read cache improves performance for data reads. It is, however, not recommended for SYSTEM, temporary (TEMP) and UNDO tablespaces due to their I/O patterns.
- As an option, the temporary tablespace (TEMP) can be created on the non-persistent drive. The non-persistent drive offers sufficient I/O performance. Note that the non-persistent disk is initialized when the VM is restarted. This is no issue for Oracle because the temporary tablespace is also re-initialized at database restart. When you create a directory structure on the non-persistent drive, it needs to exist prior to the start of Oracle. If not, Oracle cannot start.
- When deploying on the M-Series, in combination with premium storage, write latency can be reduced by using the Write Accelerator. As the name suggests, the purpose of the functionality is to improve the I/O latency of writes against Azure Premium Storage. Write Accelerator is ideally suited where log file updates are required to persist to disk, in a highly performant manner.

5.2.4 Using SAP ASE

SAP ASE (Adaptive Server Enterprise), originally known as Sybase SQL Server, and also commonly known as Sybase DB or Sybase ASE, is a relational model database server developed by the Sybase Corporation, which later became part of SAP. ASE is predominantly used on the Unix platform, but is also available for Windows.

There are not many differences between hosting SAP ASE on-premise and in the Cloud. Administration and development tools work exactly the same, and are all supported.

Recommendations for SAP ASE are as follows:

- The minimum version should be SAP ASE 16.
- The SAP ASE executables can be located on the system disk. The SAP ASE system and tools databases do not experience high

workload. Therefore, they can also remain on the system disk. This statement does not apply to the TEMPDB (temporary database). For performance reasons, it makes sense to move the TEMPDB to a dedicated disk. Never keep any SAP ASE device on the non-persistent disks, even the TEMPDB database.

- If the number of IOPS per disk satisfies your requirements, all data volumes can be installed on the same disk, and the log volumes on another disk. If more IOPS are needed, it is recommended to use Windows Storage Pools or the Linux Logical Volumes. This is much easier than manually dividing volumes among disks.
- Backing up and restoring a database in Azure works the same way as it does for on-premise systems. Backups or dumps are taken to disk. For performance reasons, you might consider using Windows Storage Pools or Linux Logical Volumes, as you would for the data and log volumes.
- Data replication can be used to increase availability. With the SAP Sybase Replication Server (SRS), SAP ASE provides a warm standby solution to transfer database changes from the primary database to the secondary database. The installation and operation of SRS works in the same way on Azure as it does on-premise. SAP ASE HADR does not require an Azure internal load balancer and has no dependencies on OS-level clustering. It works on Azure Windows and Linux VMs

5.2.5 Using SAP HANA

SAP HANA is supported on certified hardware only. In Azure, these are the virtual machines listed in the SAP Certified IaaS Platforms directory. SAP HANA is supported on Azure virtual machines up 3.8TB with 128 vCPUs.

What if you need more? Although 3.8TB is sufficient for most installations, for some large installations it is not. This is where the Large Instances come in. Basically, a Large Instance is a certified appliance in an SAP HANA Tailored Data Center Integration (TDI) setup. They are listed in the Certified IaaS Platforms directory as the S-Series. From an administration and system operations perspective, there is no difference between an SAP HANA database deployed on an Azure virtual machine and an SAP HANA database deployed on a Large Instance.

There are some significant differences, however, because there is no virtualization layer (see Figure 5.1):

- Unlike an Azure virtual machine, there is no virtualization layer or hypervisor. With the Large Instance you get the performance of the bare-metal server.
- Unlike an Azure virtual machine, a Large Instance server is dedicated to a specific customer. Failures, reboots and shutdowns result in unavailability of the SAP HANA database. Therefore, a high-availability solution such as SAP HANA replication or storage replication needs to be considered.
- Unlike with an Azure virtual machine, where host processor types are selected for the best price-performance ratio, the processor types chosen for SAP HANA on Azure (Large Instances) are the highest performing of the Intel processor line.
- Bare-metal servers are only supported to run SAP HANA. The SAP application layer needs to be deployed on standard virtual machines.

The following requirements need to be taken into account when running SAP HANA on Azure Large Instances:

- Proper sizing is needed. The Large Instance is a dedicated appliance in an SAP TDI setup. For greenfield installations, you need to use Quick Sizer. For existing systems, you can use sizing reports. Sizing is explained in detail in SAP Note 1793345—"Sizing for SAP Suite on HANA", and in SAP Note 1872170—"ABAP on HANA sizing report (S/4HANA, Suite on HANA)".
- You must have an Azure subscription. This needs to be extended with Microsoft Premium Mission Critical Support (see SAP Note 2015553—"SAP on Microsoft Azure: Support Prerequisites"). If you use SAP HANA Large Instance units with more than 384 CPUs, you also need to extend the premier support contract to include Azure Rapid Response.
- You need an Azure ExpressRoute between the systems you have deployed in Azure and those on-premise. Make sure to get at least a 1 Gbps connection from your Internet Service Provider (ISP) to connect your on-premise data center to Azure. Connectivity between the Large Instances and Azure also uses ExpressRoute

technology. This is, however, invisible to you and is included in the setup.

- For SUSE you need the SUSE Linux Subscription Management Tool (SMT) deployed in Azure on an Azure virtual machine. This provides the ability for SAP HANA on Azure (Large Instances) to be registered and updated by SUSE. For Red Hat you need the Red Hat Subscription Manager.
- SAP also requires you to have a support contract with the Linux distribution of your choice (SLES or RHEL). This is, however, your responsibility and is not included in the service cost.

SAP HANA data tiering and extension nodes are also supported on Azure Large Instances. With SAP HANA extension nodes, data can be classified as hot, warm or cold. *Hot* data is kept in-memory, on the fastest SAP HANA instance. The extension nodes hold *warm* data, and *cold* data is stored off-line in HADOOP or Sybase IQ.

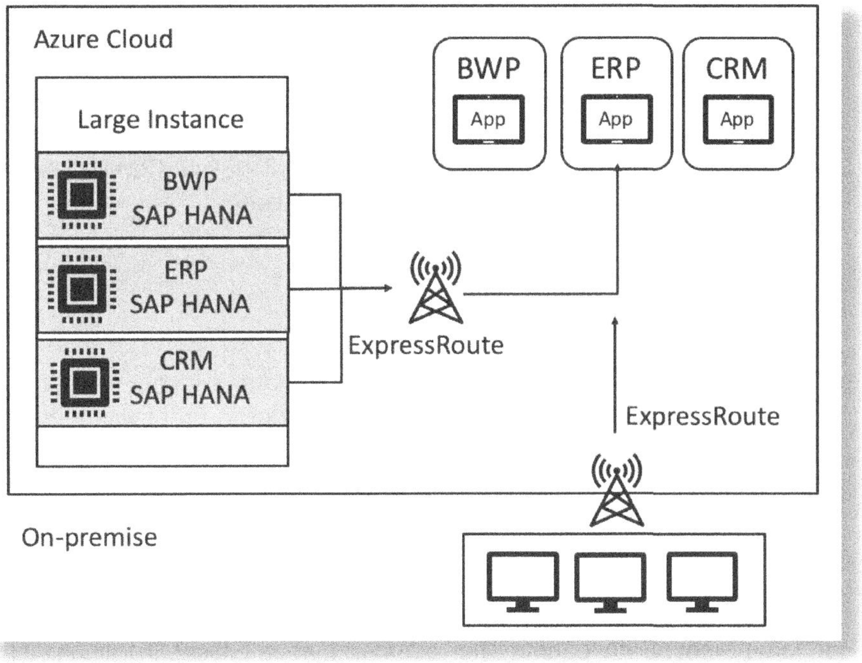

Figure 5.1: SAP HANA Large Instance layout in Microsoft Azure

System layout

The system layout of a Large Instance is as follows;

- Only the SAP HANA database is installed on the Large Instance. The Central Services Instance and application servers are deployed on regular virtual machines. The same applies to smaller SAP HANA databases for which virtual machines are perfectly suitable.
- The SAP HANA Large Instance is an SAP HANA TDI Certified Hardware installation connected to your Azure subscription using the same technology as the connection between your on-premise installation and Azure.

Storage layout for SAP HANA on Azure (Large Instance)

The storage layout for SAP HANA on Azure (Large Instance) is configured by SAP HANA on the classic deployment model, as per SAP recommended guidelines. As with Certified Appliances, Microsoft provisions the Large Instance for you and links it to your Azure subscription. There is an intake procedure to follow in which you provide Microsoft with the desired hostname, IP-address, SID, etc. Note that you need to install SAP HANA yourself. This differs from classic Certified Appliances. These come with SAP HANA pre-installed.

Storage recommendations

When working with Certified Appliances, the storage layout is important, and this is taken care of by the hardware vendor in on-premise installations. You only need to supply your hardware vendor with the expected SAP HANA memory footprint, and they can do the calculations to come up with a suitable storage layout.

In the Cloud, you need to build your infrastructure yourself and you should be aware that although SAP HANA is an in-memory database, save points and in-memory data loading after a restart can be critical.

Recommendations for running SAP HANA on virtual machines are as follows:

- Use premium disks for the `/hana/data` and `/hana/log` volumes.
- To increase performance, consider using Logical Volumes. Performance on disk is limited by the maximum number of IOPS the disk can deliver. You can use Logical Volumes to overcome that limit. For example, a volume on four P40 disks gives you four times the IOPS of a single P40 disk. You can use RAID-0 for these volumes. You don't need to configure storage redundancy because premium storage is kept threefold in Azure.
- Read caching is not recommended on SAP HANA data files. There is hardly any read workload against the data files. An exception is when the SAP HANA instance is started, or during a database backup. Read caching in these instances makes no sense because the data file needs to be read completely anyway.
- Write caching is also not recommended. Writing is only done during save points or crash recovery. Save points are written asynchronously and do not block other transactions. I/O performance is only critical during crash recovery, which should only be in exceptional circumstances.
- Read caching is also not recommended for log files. Log files are only read during transaction log backups and crash recovery. The main load against the SAP HANA log file are writes. Although write performance is critical, all writes need to be persisted on disk immediately for data-consistency and crash-recovery purposes. Therefore, write caching is also not recommended.
- The SAP HANA executables and configuration files are stored in the `/hana/shared` directory. The directory is shared between all SAP HANA hosts in the case of a distributed SAP HANA system. Read caching may be considered, but it does not have a significant performance impact.

The Azure Write Accelerator for the M-Series

The Write Accelerator is a new functionality which comes with the M-Series. It improves I/O latency of writes against premium storage. Tests have shown that it makes sense to use it against the `/hana/log` volume.

High availability

Microsoft supports the SAP HANA out-of-the-box high-availability methods, which include:

- **Storage replication**—this is the ability for the storage system itself to replicate all data to another location, either within the same data center, or a separate one. SAP HANA operates independently from this method. Storage replication can only be used in an SAP TDI setup or in Azure, with Large Instances. This functionality is the default disaster-recovery mechanism offered for SAP HANA Large Instances.
- **System replication**—this involves replication of all data in SAP HANA to a separate SAP HANA system. RTO and RPO are minimized by performing data replication at regular intervals. SAP HANA supports asynchronous, synchronous in-memory, and synchronous modes. The setup in Azure does not differ much from the setup in an on-premise installation. It consists of two identical virtual machines in the same availability set or zone, a load balancer, and an SLES Failover Cluster. The SLES cluster is based on the Pacemaker framework, in conjunction with a STONITH device. The Pacemaker framework contains a heartbeat daemon and a Cluster Resource Manager, which has start and stop services. STONITH is a technique to protect the cluster—it stands for "shoot the other node in the head. The STONITH device is made to do just that, powering down a node that is not working correctly.
- Host Auto-Failover—one or more standby SAP HANA nodes are configured in scale-out mode, and SAP HANA automatically fails over to another node when the master node becomes unavailable. Host Auto-Failover is only used in scale-out SAP HANA installations. Scale-out in Azure is supported with SAP HANA Large Instances and SAP HANA on virtual machines.

Scale-out limitations with virtual machines

Standby nodes cannot be used because Azure virtual machines have no native NFS service.

There are different options to implement SAP HANA high-availability features in the Cloud, and they differ in RPO, RTO, setup and running costs. These options are:

- **SAP HANA auto-restart**—this is the most straightforward option. SAP HANA is installed in a single VM. There is no system replication. When the virtual machine fails, it is automatically restarted on a different host. Because auto-restart is set for the SAP HANA instance, the SAP HANA instance is restarted automatically. High availability in SAP HANA scale-out installations is based on the auto-healing of virtual machines and the SAP HANA auto-restart.
- **SAP HANA system replication with automatic failover**—this is the most common scenario. It consists of two VMs running on an SLES or RHEL Failover Cluster. This option is applicable to Large Instances and virtual machines. When used with virtual machines, they need to be part of the same availability set (see Figure 5.2). The SLES or RHEL cluster is based on the Pacemaker framework, in conjunction with a STONITH device. SAP HANA replication is configured in synchronous replication, and automatic failover is active. The standby node receives a synchronous stream of change records from the primary SAP HANA instance. The primary SAP HANA node does not confirm the write to the application until the secondary SAP HANA node confirms that it has received the change and written it to disk. The secondary node acts as a hot standby. As of SAP HANA 2.0, the database can be configured in an active/active mode.

Hot vs cold standby vs active/active

An SAP HANA standby database can be operated in several ways. A hot standby has all data in memory and is ready to take over immediately. The same applies to a cold standby. However, data is not fully loaded into memory, meaning that there will be a performance impact when the standby has to take over from the primary because data has to be loaded from disk to memory. The advantage of a cold standby is that it has a small memory footprint. The system on which it runs can be shared with a non-production system such as an acceptance or development system. When a failover is needed, the non-production systems is halted, allowing the cold standby to allocate all memory available. Active/active is available as of SAP HANA 2.0. In an active/active mode, work is divided among both nodes, primary and standby. The standby is no longer idle and waiting for something to happen. Write transactions are always sent to the primary node, and read transactions are divided between both primary and secondary nodes.

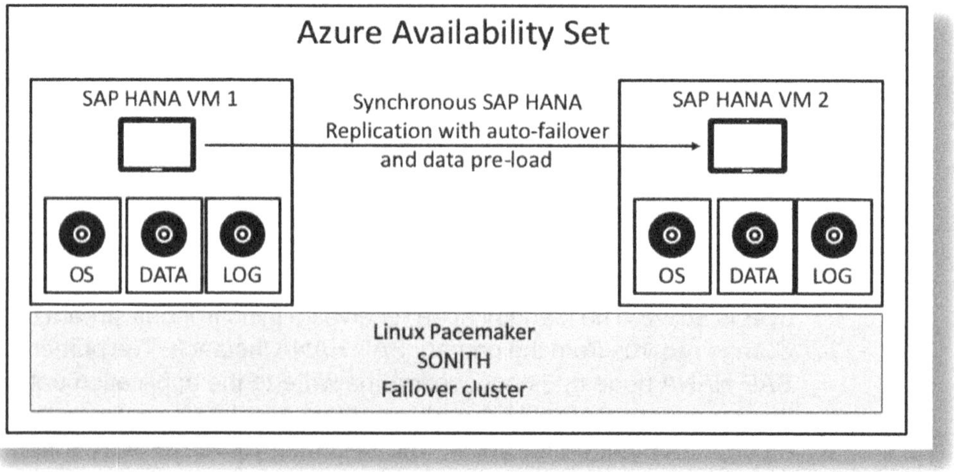

Figure 5.2: SAP HANA high-availability layout in Azure

- **System replication without auto-failover and without data pre-load**—in this setup, data is synchronously replicated to the secondary SAP HANA database in order to achieve an RPO of 0. RTO is higher because, at failover, data needs to be loaded into memory. Data is not pre-loaded, so a smaller virtual machine for the primary SAP HANA database can be used. Both virtual machines need to reside in the same availability set. This significantly reduces cost because in the Cloud, you pay for what you use. The virtual machine needs to be resized before the failover and it might take some time before the database becomes available; this is because data needs to be loaded into memory. RTO is much higher than with auto-failover and data preload.

- **Replicate backups to a second virtual machine**—in this setup the database and transaction log backup are shipped from one VM to another. You are responsible for scripting the copy of the backups from the first VM to the second. On the second VM, you also need to script the restoration of the backup and the application of the log backups yourself. In addition to protecting yourself from a hardware failure, backup replication to a second virtual machine can also be used to protect against logical mistakes such as the accidental deletion of data or tables if the backups are not immediately applied to the secondary database. The downside of this solution is an increased RTO because, in the case of a failover, a number of backups might need to be applied before all data is available.
- **SAP HANA availability across Azure Regions** (see Figure 5.3)—availability can be increased by installing a third SAP HANA database in another Azure Region. Depending on geopolitical area, the distance between regions can be hundreds, or sometimes thousands, of miles. Synchronous replication is not an option between Azure Regions due to the network latency. SAP introduced multi-target system replication with SAP HANA 2.0 SPS3. Advantages of multi-target replication include high-availability and disaster-recovery scenarios. Replicating changes from the primary database to a secondary database, and from the secondary to a third database has existed for some time. The disadvantage of this queued replication is that the last database in the queue can be impacted when the secondary database is down for maintenance and updates. This is no longer an issue with multi-target system replication.

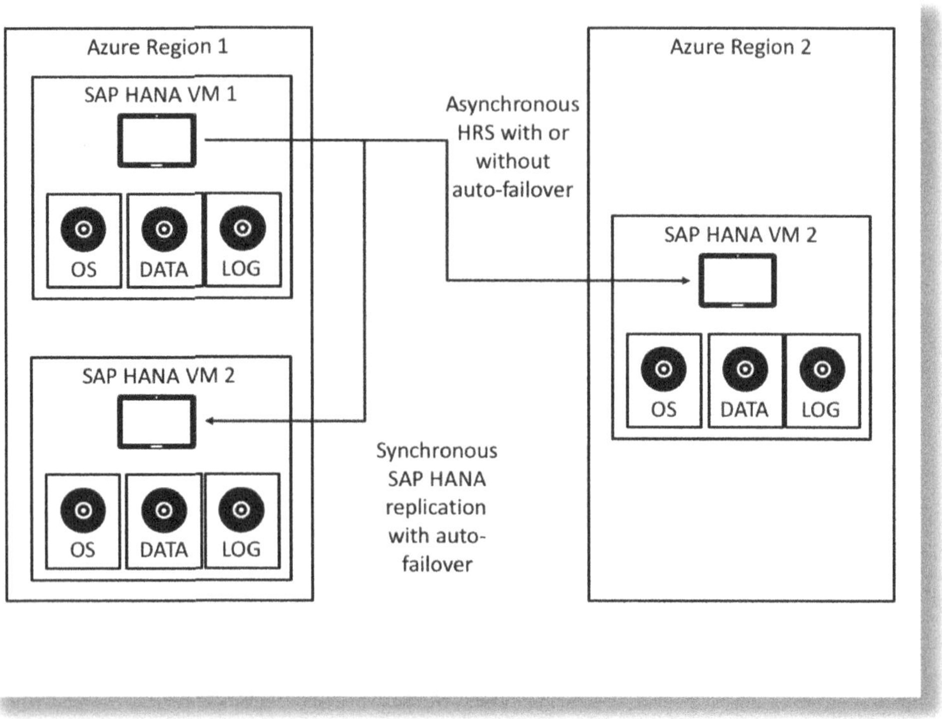

Figure 5.3: High availability across regions

Scale-up and scale-out

With SAP HANA, scalability can be either scale-up or scale-out (see Figure 5.4). Scale-up is straightforward—just add capacity. Increase memory, CPU and storage as needed, or up to the hardware limit of the SAP HANA appliance. If the hardware limit is reached, move your SAP HANA to a new, larger appliance.

Scale-up is currently limited to 24 TB of memory but this limit will probably already have been exceeded by the time you read this book.

Please note that the scale-up server hardware for OLAP applications, such as SAP Business Warehouse, differs from server hardware for OLTP applications, such as SAP Business Suite powered by SAP HANA products. The amount of memory is always related to the amount of CPU cores. For OLTP applications, more RAM per CPU core is possible.

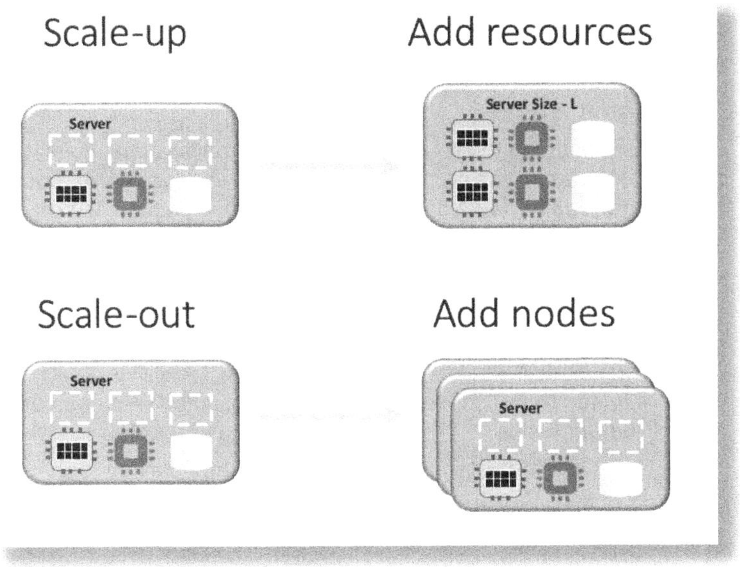

Figure 5.4: Scale-up versus scale-out

A scale-out system consists of separate SAP HANA servers or nodes, linked together. Data is distributed across the nodes and each node takes care of the data processing. An advantage of scale-out is built-in high availability. One or several nodes can be configured as standby. If one of the nodes fails, the standby takes over the data of the failed node and continues processing. As soon as the failed node is available again, it can be re-integrated into the system layout as standby.

Table 5.2 compares scale-up and scale-out solutions.

	Scale-up	**Scale-out**
Support	Every SAP component supported on SAP HANA is supported in a scale-up layout.	Limited (see SAP Note 1825774—"SAP Business Suite Powered by SAP HANA - Multi-Node Support" for detailed information).
Consolidation	Multiple SAP HANA databases can be consolidated on a single SAP HANA system.	Only one SAP HANA database per system.

	Scale-up	Scale-out
Complexity	Simple and straightforward.	Complex, due to cross-node communication and data distribution.
Cost	Depends on the resource requirements. The higher the requirements, the higher the cost.	Several smaller appliances might be less expensive, but maintenance costs could be more expensive.
Skills	Limited—a scale-up solution does not provide table and load distribution, or hash algorithms.	SAP HANA knowledge is needed to properly distribute data among the different nodes.
Growth	Limited to the capacity of the appliance.	Almost unlimited—nodes can be added as needed.
High availability	SAP HANA system replication or via shared storage using one worker + one standby configuration.	Scale-out has built-in, high availability capabilities through the use of one or more standby nodes.

Table 5.2: Comparison of scale-up and scale-out solutions

Larger, single SAP HANA systems (scale-up) are more expensive but are easier to manage than scale-out systems that have distributed data and multiple nodes.

There are several limits when implementing SAP HANA scale-out on Azure which need to be taken into account. These are:

- On Azure, only the M-Series is certified for scale-out on virtual machines. The S-Series is supported for scale-out on Large Instances. The minimum operating system version is SUSE Linux 12 SP3 and Red Hat Linux 7.4.
- Standby nodes cannot be used because Azure virtual machines have no native NFS service. The NFS needs to be set up using operating system functionality which does not match the storage latency criteria of SAP HANA. Because of this, the data and log volumes cannot be shared, which is the basic requirement for standby nodes.
- Scale-out is certified up to 16 nodes, with one node as the master node and a maximum of 15 worker nodes.

A basic configuration of a scale-out installation on Azure has the following layout (see Figure 5.5):

- All binary, trace and configuration files are stored in file system `/hana/shared`. The file system is shared between all SAP HANA nodes.
- The shared file system can have high availability by installing a highly available NFS cluster. So far, the highly available NFS cluster works only with SUSE Linux. The NFS cluster consists of two virtual machines residing in the same availability set. The NFS cluster uses a dedicated virtual hostname and IP address. An Azure load balancer is required to failover the virtual host name and IP address. The Distributed Replicated Block Device (DRBD) is used to keep the file system in sync between the two nodes.
- The `/hana/data` and `/hana/log` volumes are not shared. Every node has its own data and log volume.

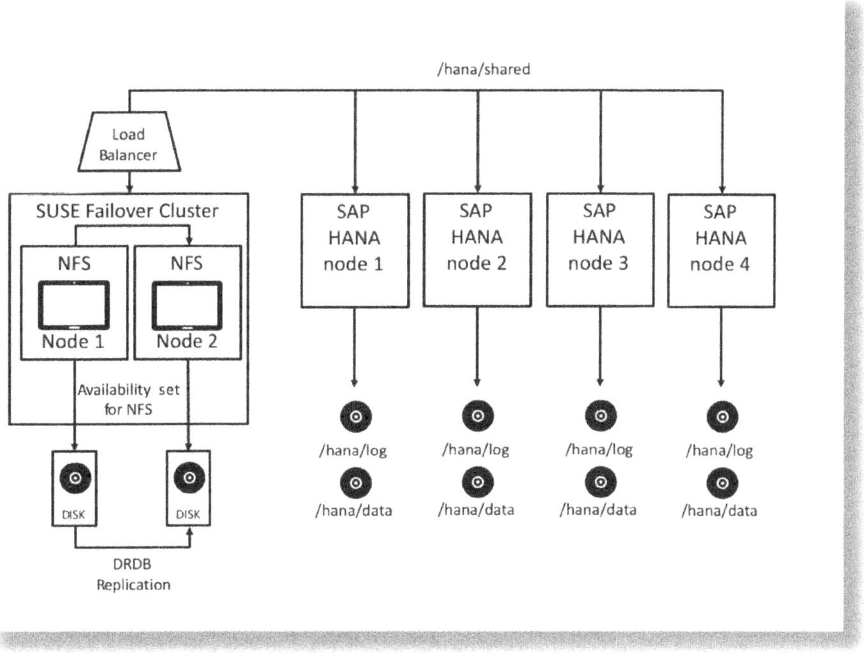

Figure 5.5: SAP HANA scale-out on Azure

Backup and recovery

The following SAP HANA backup options exist by default:

- Backup to the file system—this option exists with many database systems and is straightforward. The database is written to a database dump file on a local filesystem. The dump file can then be stored to Azure Blob Storage in a second step. Another option is to write the backup on a shared filesystem which resides in another virtual machine. In the second option, the virtual machine can be backed up using the Azure Backup Service.
- Backup using storage snapshots to the Azure storage blob, using the Azure Backup Service—the database should be aware that a storage snapshot is being taken. If the database is warned, it can save a consistent state to disk before the snapshot is taken. This is needed in order to guarantee data consistency. For more information on storage snapshots, see SAP Note 2039883—"FAQ: SAP HANA database and storage snapshots". Storage snapshots are supported with SAP HANA running on a virtual machine, and with SAP HANA on Azure Large Instances.

5.2.6 Using SQL Server

SQL Server is a very popular database among SAP customers. In combination with SAP, SQL Server 2008 R2 and higher is supported on Azure.

Recommendations for an SQL Server on Azure are the same as for on-premise. They are as follows:

- The SQL Server executables should be located on the system drive. Typically, most of the SQL Server system databases are not utilized at a high level by SAP workload. As a result, the SQL Server system databases (Master, MSDB, and Model) can remain on the system drive as well.
- The TEMPDB can be deployed on the non-persistent drive because it is recreated every time SQL Server restarts. Note that when you create a directory structure on the non-persistent drive, it needs to exist prior to the start of SQL Server. If not, SQL Server cannot start.

- Storage recommendations do not differ between bare metal and virtual. It is recommended to separate the data from the database logs, and to use one storage pool for the data files and a separate storage pool for the transaction log file. Storage pools enable you to overcome the maximum number of IOPS a single disk can deliver by combining several disks in one pool.
- Database performance is almost always related to the storage layout. We therefore strongly recommend premium storage. Performance can be improved by enabling read caching for the data files. Disk caching is not recommended for the transaction log.
- When deploying on the M-Series, in combination with premium storage, write latency can be reduced by using the Write Accelerator. As the name suggests, the purpose of the functionality is to improve the I/O latency of writes against Azure Premium Storage. The Write Accelerator is ideally suited because log file updates are required to persist to disk in a highly performant way.
- Different solutions exist for backup and recovery: Automated Backup for SQL Server, Azure Backup for SQL Server VM and manual backup to disk or Blog Storage.
  - Automatic Backup is an automated backup service. It enables you to configure regular backups using Azure Blob Storage.
  - Backup for SQL Server VM uses the SQL Server VSS/VDI Interface to stream backups to a target location; in this case, the Azure Recovery Services vault.
  - Manual backups can be taken to attached disks or directly to an Azure Blob Storage (backup via URL).
- High availability can be achieved via SQL Server clustering, log shipping, database mirroring and always on. Although these solutions are comparable to their on-premise counterparts, there are some Azure specifics to consider. The different solutions are explained in detail in the Microsoft documentation, which is available at: *https://docs.microsoft.com/en-us/azure/virtual-machines/workloads/sap/dbms_guide_sqlserver*
- Be careful when using an SQL Server image from Azure Marketplace. Microsoft offers virtual machines with a pre-installed version of SQL Server. This might be an opportunity for customers who did do not get their SQL Server license via SAP, but via Microsoft

directly. You should however take the following considerations into account:

- You can only use SQL Server versions supported by SAP. For SAP NetWeaver, this is the Enterprise Edition. This is a requirement, even for non-production systems.
- The collation of the SQL Server instance, which is installed by default, is not the collation SAP NetWeaver requires in order to run. This needs to be adapted before SAP installation can proceed.

6 Design guidelines

So far, we have discussed the different components of Azure that are useful in an SAP context. We have covered installation options and guidelines, high availability, and disaster recovery. Before we jump into transformation, migration, and a customer example, we want to run through some design guidelines for performance, security, availability and recoverability, and cost savings.

6.1 Design for performance

Use premium storage for the SAP database server in order to benefit from high-performance and low-latency I/O, especially for production and heavily used non-production systems. We have seen customer cases where the development system was considered to be as important as the production system, particularly during the roll-out of new projects. You need to verify the maximum I/O you can get from a single SSD disk against your requirements. You may need to build a RAID-0 stripe to increase the maximum number of IOPS. Standard SSD or HDD can be used for non-production systems or for the SAP and RDBMS executables. HDD storage is, in most cases, sufficient for backup storage.

You should take advantage of the virtual machines which support accelerated networking. With accelerated networking, all networking policies are applied to the hardware instead of the virtual switch. Applying network policies to hardware enables the network interface (NIC) to forward network traffic directly to the VM, bypassing the host and the virtual switch, while maintaining the policy it applied in the host.

When running your SAP database on the M-Series, enable Write Accelerator on your database log volumes to improve write I/O latency. Write Accelerator is mandatory for productive SAP HANA workloads to ensure a low write latency to the `/hana/log` volume.

6.2 Design for security

The on-premise Active Directory can be extended to the Cloud. For full cloud, the Azure Active Directory (Azure AD) can be used. Single Sign-On (SSO) can be enabled on your Fiori launchpad in both cases. Azure AD can also be integrated with the SAP Cloud Platform (SCP) to provide SSO to the applications deployed there.

Take time to configure the Network Security Groups (NSG). NSGs allow you to filter network traffic to and from your virtual network. Rules should be defined to enable access to your SAP services, thereby denying access to other services.

For data security, Azure Disk Encryption can be used to encrypt disks where the operating system, SAP and database executables, and data and log volumes are stored. Database backups can be encrypted as well.

6.3 Design for availability and recoverability

Use availability sets for critical SAP systems in order to protect components such as the SAP Central Services (SCS) and the database server. Configure operating system cluster technologies such as Windows Failover Cluster or Linux Pacemaker. Set up database replication between the primary and secondary database servers to ensure no loss of data. For the SAP Application Servers, configure at least two in the same availability set. Availability can be increased by deploying systems in availability zones. Availability sets are configured within one data center, and zones are configured within one Azure Region, thereby protecting components against a full data-center failure.

Recoverability can be increased further by using Azure Paired Regions (see Figure 6.1). Azure Paired Regions protect against the loss of a complete Azure Region in situations such as a largescale disaster or civil unrest. Using paired regions increases complexity and cost. It is therefore necessary to understand the RPO and RTO. The setup needs to be extended with asynchronous database replication to an additional standby system. Virtual machines need to be protected by Azure Site Recovery.

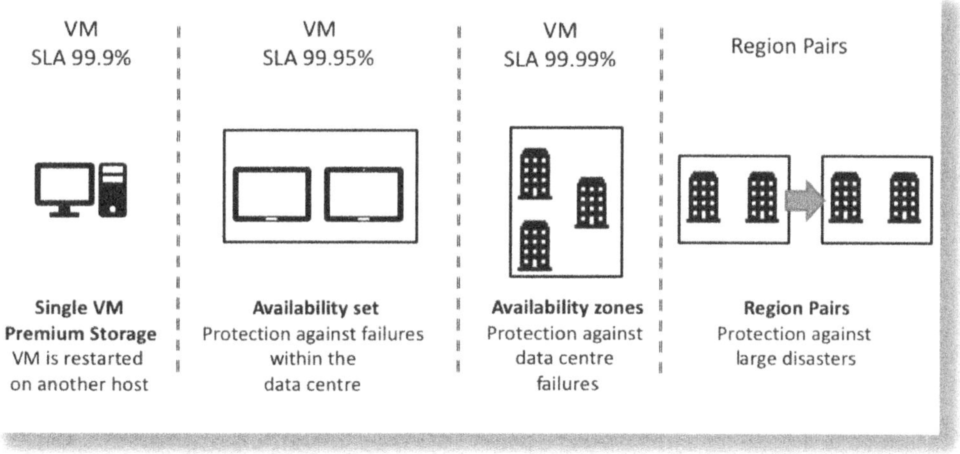

Figure 6.1: Increased high-availability using regions

6.4 Design for cost saving

It is a misconception that the public cloud is always less expensive than bare metal or a private cloud. It might be, if you use the public cloud cleverly. By running your SAP workload on Azure, you avoid CAPEX (capital expenditure) but increase OPEX (operational expenditure).

OPEX can be reduced in the following ways:

- Use reserved instances for your 24/7 systems. Reserved instances can reduce the VM costs by up to 70%. Reserving a VM does not mean that you get stuck with that particular VM for the reserved time period. You actually get a reservation for the VM size group. A VM size group is a group of VMs with the same size attributes. For example, if you reserve a VM Standard_DS5_v2, you get the reservation discount for all the VMs in the group (Standard_DS1_v2, Standard_DS2_v2, Standard_DS3_v2, and Standard_DS4_v2). Let's say you reserve a VM instance with the size Standard_DS4_v2, where the ratio or relative footprint compared to the other sizes within the group is 8:
  - Scenario 1—run eight Standard_DS1_v2-sized VMs with a ratio of 1. Your reservation discount applies to all eight of those VMs.
  - Scenario 2—run two Standard_DS2_v2-sized VMs with a ratio of 2 each. In addition, run a Standard_DS3_v2-sized VM with a ratio of 4. The total footprint is 2+2+4=8. So your reservation discount applies to all three of those VMs.
  - Scenario 3—run one Standard_DS5_v2 with a ratio of 16. Your reservation discount applies to half of that VM's compute cost.
- Do you really need availability sets or zones for all your production systems? They increase availability, but also cost and complexity. Remember that Azure offers 99.9% availability for a single VM.
- Use scale-on demand. If you can predict the load of your SAP systems over a longer time period, scale-on demand allows you to

add additional compute power during month-end, year-end, payroll processing, etc.

- De-allocating or "snoozing" virtual machines brings tremendous cost savings. Remember that with pay-as-you-go, you pay for what you use. In many organizations non-production systems are only used during the week. You configure the snooze schedule once and Azure takes care of the stop/start of the VMs. The databases are normally restarted automatically. The same can be achieved for the SAP components by enabling the Autostart parameter.
- Carefully select the region. You would normally select the region which is closest to your on-premise systems in order to avoid network latency. Region selection can also be dependent on compliance requirements, such as the EU General Data Protection Regulation (GDPR). If more than one region applies to your requirements, compare the prices of compute resources; some might be cheaper than other regions.
- Use SAP HANA-certified virtual machines for production. This is, however, not needed for non-production systems such as development, acceptance demo, etc. Because performance tends to be less critical on non-production systems, you might even consider using smaller virtual machines.
- Select your storage wisely. Premium SSD is more expensive than standard SSD or HDD. Use standard SSD for non-production systems. Standard HDD is sufficient for storing backup dumps.

7 Prepare your transformation

SAP is available for many different hardware platforms and database systems. Over time, you may need to change your operating system or database for various reasons.

In today's economy, where companies are constantly being bought and sold, platform and database migrations happen more than you can imagine. IT departments are constantly looking for ways to reduce costs. Standardization is one way to achieve this. Most of the time, the IT infrastructure of a company that has been bought needs to be adapted to the one taking over. Another important reason for doing platform migrations is that reliability of the hardware or software vendor is at stake. Who remembers Informix or True Unix? Both were strong platforms, but they are now long gone. You might also choose another hardware platform or database system because the current infrastructure is reaching its limits and has to be replaced before the next SAP upgrade. And finally, by 2025, every SAP customer will have to be migrated to SAP HANA.

These types of projects are always underestimated. From a business perspective, they are considered a waste of time and need to be done as quickly as possible with a minimum amount of resources and costs. Although system administrators might argue otherwise, one should realize that, from a business perspective, there's no real benefit from a platform migration. Performance might improve and operating costs might be reduced, but SAP remains SAP. Migration projects bring no new functionality. This explains why companies are less willing to release resources and budget for a platform migration than for other projects. In most of situations, they are considered an extra step in an SAP upgrade project because new hardware needs to be installed to support the new SAP release, or they are part of a company's worldwide standardization project. And let's be honest, don't we all assume that SAP is operating system and database independent?

SAP data is database independent and tools exist to download your data to binary files and upload them again in another database on another platform. Unfortunately, these tools are not so straightforward. In addition, there's the burden of migrating all the tools and scripts you implemented or developed over the years. All this, together with all external system interfaces, needs to be reviewed. Your ABAP developers are impacted as well. Although not recommended by SAP, many customers use specific SQL (database dependent) commands in their ABAP programs. Needless to say, all these need to be reexamined and rewritten during the migration as well. Last but not least, all ABAP custom code needs to be reviewed when migrating to SAP HANA. Most tables in SAP HANA are kept in a column store. There are rules regarding which customer code ABAP needs to comply with in order to function as expected on SAP HANA.

Fortunately, SAP provides you with the OS/DB Migration Service. The migration service provides assistance and know-how for migrations. The service includes templates, sample project plans, SAP migration tools, and SAP GoingLive Check. When migrating production systems from one operating system or database to another, the OS/DB Migration Service is mandatory; SAP only supports you during the course of the project if you use the service. In addition, SAP requires you to carry out the migration in close collaboration with a certified migration partner, or consulting firm, with the necessary migration expertise. The OS/DB Migration Service is applicable to all SAP versions and all databases and operating systems supported by SAP. A migration to the Cloud is considered heterogenous if the operating system and/or database changes during the migration. If you move from an on-premise installation to a cloud installation, but the operating systems and database remains the same, it is considered a homogeneous migration and the service is not needed.

7.1 Project phases

A migration or transformation project can be divided into three logical phases:

- Phase 1—preparation phase. This phase begins with a decision to undertake a migration, and ends with the project plan.
- Phase 2—migration phase. This is where most of the work is done. This phase starts with the very first test migration and ends with the migration of the production system.
- Phase 3—follow-up. The final phase begins when all systems have been migrated and includes several follow-up activities.

The following section provides an overview of the steps that are executed in each phase.

7.1.1 Phase 1—Preparation

All wishes and requirements are discussed in the preparation phase. Expectations need to be appropriately set so that they can be met in the planning and execution of the activities.

The project starts with a decision to migrate to another operating system or database, instead of remaining on the current one. This is particularly the case for customers not running on Windows or Linux, because only these two are supported on Azure. Experience shows that this decision is a very difficult one to make, and in most cases takes longer than the migration project itself. All the pros and cons need to be taken into account. The cost and effort of the migration should be carefully compared against the new platform's license and support fees, especially if cost reduction is the main objective. Regarding cost and effort, you shouldn't only look at the migration itself; many tools which communicate with the SAP system might also need to be reviewed. Significant time and effort has to go into training IT staff as well.

A platform migration means new hardware or infrastructure. An OS migration always goes to new systems. There is no new OS if there is no new hardware. But for database migrations, new hardware is also needed. SAP does not support any migration in which the source system and target system are the same. New hardware is needed for the test migrations anyway. You should be able to configure the new environment while the production system continues running. After the live migration, SAP requires the old production system to continue running for at least a few weeks, just for reference. This means that you have two SAP landscapes during the course of the project, the new and the old.

Although the administration load swiftly shifts from the old to the new environment, you should not underestimate the impact of the temporary system increase. More systems mean more daily administration, more backups, and so on.

In the Cloud, hardware is at your fingertips. There is no delay in ordering, assembling and connecting hardware. However, do not underestimate the time needed to design the infrastructure in the Cloud. True, in the Cloud, virtual machines, storage and networking are only a click away, but enough time should be taken to think about performance, scalability, high availability and disaster recovery.

The first step in the project is the easiest. Contact SAP about your intention to migrate. In return, SAP will send you information on how to proceed, as well as a migration questionnaire. Beforehand, you might want to consult the OS/DB migration white papers and documentation at *https://support.sap.com/en/offerings-programs/support-services/os-db-migration-check.html* (you will need to log on to the SAP Support Portal to access this information).

SAP then sends a contract, the SAP Agreement for the OS/DB Migration Service. The contract specifies the requirements and contractual obligations of both SAP and the customer. Contractual arrangements also need to be made for the license change, otherwise it is not possible for SAP to deliver an installation package for the new operating system and/or database (OS/DB).

You need to establish a migration project plan with your consulting partner. Based on this plan, fill in the questionnaire you received earlier and send it to SAP. SAP assesses the project based on the submitted questionnaire. They then approve or reject the project based on the number of test migrations, the time between test and live migration, and whether the migration partner is certified or not. In the questionnaire, you should indicate when you would like the GoingLive Check to take place in the source and target systems, both before and after the migration. By default, there will be two GoingLive sessions in the source system and one after the new system goes live. If approved by SAP, you can proceed to the next step.

How much time do we need for this phase?

This phase can take quite some time, even though it is only a preparation phase. Many different parties are involved, and a new architecture needs to be designed in the Cloud. Some training might also be needed in order to become acquainted with the different technological capabilities. The setup of a dedicated network connection between the on-premise installation and Azure could also take time; it needs to be ordered, installed and connected. This can take several weeks or more.

A new contract for your future OS/DB platform, and for the OS/DB migration service, needs to be signed. You need to take the availability of your migration partner into account as well. A project plan needs to be established, which might depend on business requirements. Don't forget that you will need some downtime during the final cutover weekend. SAP recommends starting three to four months before the first actual migration. Even if no hardware change is involved, two months would be an absolute minimum.

7.1.2 Phase 2—Migration

This is a repetitive phase, consisting of several migrations—one or more test migrations, migrations of the critical non-production systems, and finally the migration of the production system. The test migrations are repeated as many times as needed, until you are confident enough with the migration procedure to tackle the production system:

- First test migration—in most projects, this is the migration of the development system. It enables you to learn the behavior of the tools in your environment, identify and solve problems that arise, and document the process. This migration therefore takes longer than subsequent migrations, even if it is carried out on a relatively small system. For operating system migrations, when the new development system becomes productive, the shared transport directory might need to be shared between different operating systems. This is supported, but should be considered before the new system replaces the old one.

- When doing a database migration, you should consider an extra migration using a sandbox system. The sandbox system should be a copy of the production system. Having a system which has the same size as the production system is very useful from a performance and tuning perspective. The migration needs to be tuned to reduce downtime. You need to exercise the migration procedure on the sandbox system until you reduce the runtime of the migration to an acceptable level. It might also be useful to take additional time to learn the architecture and behavior of the new database system. Don't forget that your ABAP developers will need time to verify and adapt all their code, modifying any which have hard-coded, SQL-dependent commands, or which, when migrating to SAP HANA, do not fulfill the SAP HANA strict code requirements.
- Second test migration—this could be done on a copy of the production system; for example, quality assurance or on the production system itself, if possible. The choice between the quality assurance or production system depends on two factors. The first factor is how long ago the quality assurance was refreshed from production. Testing the migration procedure on a very old copy of production does not provide enough information to enable you to estimate the time needed for the migration of the production system. The second factor is downtime. Don't forget that SAP is not available during the export of the source database. This might be difficult in 24/7 businesses, and it might be wise to refresh quality assurance before using it in order to test the migration. The migration will reveal new problems which are related to the production environment, but the main aim of this test is to estimate the required run time in production, and to fine-tune the migration performance.
- Other test migrations—we repeat the scenario until we achieve a migration downtime that is at a level acceptable to the different business units.
- Between the different test migrations, the newly installed systems need to be extensively tested. Many people from different organizations need to be involved in these tests, and they should approve or reject the new environment before it goes live. ABAP developers might need some time to test their developments. This might take

more time in the database than in OS migration projects, especially if the developers use database-dependent SQL commands (using EXEC SQL) in their ABAP programs. For OS migrations, ABAP developers should check for any external commands or programs used in their ABAP programs.

Customer developments and SAP HANA

When migrating to SAP HANA, customer developments need to be verified and adapted where necessary. In general, all ABAP code running on SAP HANA runs just as it does on any other database. However, ABAP code which relies on specific database features or capabilities needs to be reviewed. Standard SAP code is SAP HANA-compliant. However, customer developments need to be verified. For more information, see the white paper "Best Practice Guide - Considerations for Custom ABAP Code During a Migration to SAP HANA". This is available at *https://archive.sap.com/documents/docs/DOC-46714*.

- Key users from each business unit should verify the different application modules (FI, CO, PM). They should run some performance-heavy business reports (e.g., monthly closing) to test data integrity and give an indication of the new environment's performance. For the live migration of the production instance, key users should run some business reports both before and after the migration, in both the source and the target systems. The results should be the same in both systems. The migration will only be approved if these reports have been run.

The infrastructure design

A migration project always includes a design phase. The target infrastructure is determined in this phase. The following list contains all items which should be considered in this phase:

- You should spend time on the future layout, especially for database migrations. Table space sizes, tables residing in their own table spaces, and table fragmentation should all be taken into account, particularly when migrating from table-space-oriented databases (Oracle and DB2) to database systems which don't have a table space concept (SQL Server, MaxDB or SAP HANA), or visa-versa. You should discuss this with your migration consultant at an early stage of the project.

- The configuration of your SAP system, the number of applications servers, the distribution of dialog, batch and spool processes, instances dedicated to RFC (Remote Function Call), and logon-groups, all need to be considered. It is recommended to duplicate the same environment on the new platform. We can fine-tune and possibly remove some application servers after we have the first performance figures from the new environment. If duplicating the environment is not possible, you can risk doing the same amount of work with fewer application servers. The new environment will be more performant anyway. In addition, deploying new application servers is much easier in the Cloud than in an on-premise environment.
- The printer configuration needs to be adapted for the operating system. The impact is minimal if an external output management tool, or a remote print server, is used. If you're using local host printing, it might be the right time to review your output management strategy. If not, you might end up recreating all printers at OS level on the new host.
- For both operating system migrations and database migrations, you should review all the scripts you created over the previous years. In an OS migration, you might need to re-write them all. In particular, scripts used for FTP (File Transfer Protocol) should be carefully checked because they can have a serious impact on your business. In my experience, every SAP business has some sort of anonymous FTP or SFTP (Secure File Transfer Protocol), using scripts developed in-house.
- If used, integration with high-availability software needs to be set up. High availability needs to be rigorously tested and documented. All scenarios need to be considered; hardware failures, network failures and, last but not least, software failures should be tested and documented. Take into account that a high-availability setup is completely different in a cloud environment.

- This might be a good time to establish a backup strategy and an integration with the storage manager, and to extensively test and document the different backup/recovery scenarios.
- Review your RFC connections and background environment. Although I would advise against it, many customers specify a background host in their jobs. In addition, verify the logical commands and check whether their physical counterpart should be changed to the new operating system.
- Don't forget to install the SAP agents and to configure the integration with SAP Solution Manager.
- Verify the integration with any third-party software you are using with any hierarchical storage manager you use for your archiving, and with any tools used for faxing. In addition, verify integration with Exchange, Office 365 and Opentext.
- During the different migrations, SAP performs GoingLive Check on the source system. Their recommendations should be reviewed and, if applicable, implemented.
- Copy the entire profile parameters specific for your environment (default client, logon language). These need to be copied to the new profiles on the new environment. Copying technical settings, such as memory parameters, makes no sense. The amount of memory on the target environment will, in most cases, be totally different to that on the source.
- Be prepared to change all the end users' SAP logons to the new system. This is not an issue if you have an automatic software distributor, but becomes a big issue if you don't. You might try to send every user an e-mail with new INI files attached and ask them to copy these to the correct directory. Your helpdesk will most likely be overwhelmed by end users calling for assistance.
- Last but not least, don't forget to generate a new license key for your migrated SAP systems.

How much time do we need for this phase?

Timing is dependent on the number of migrations, available resources, and time allocated for testing, etc. Between the final test migration and the migration of the production system, there should be minimum of three to four weeks. During this time, the system is thoroughly tested, and the GoingLive Check takes place (you could also migrate the development and/or quality assurance system during this time). SAP will not agree to a period of less than two weeks between final test and production. This is taken into account in the planning proposed to SAP in the questionnaire.

7.1.3 Phase 3—Follow-up

Be ready to receive an abundance of end user calls in the days following the migration of the production system. They won't just be calling to thank you for the improved response time on the new environment. They will be calling because they cannot connect, their SAP Logon was not adapted, or they can't print. Batch jobs might abort because some ABAP programs slipped through the test phases and still contain OS-specific or DB-specific statements. It might be wise to add temporary resources to your helpdesk and to have some of your ABAP developers on site.

After the migration of the production system, there is one more verification session by SAP, three to four weeks after the live migration

Don't forget that the old production system should remain active until six weeks after the migration of the production system, for reference purposes. This is an SAP requirement.

7.2 Project plan

The project plan discussed here is a guide and should be adapted to your situation to take any reasonable changes and delays into account. Also note that all the dates shown in the examples are only meant to provide an estimate of a potential timeline and are relative to the project start date.

Task Name	Duration	Start	Finish	Predecessors	Resource Names
Preparation Phase	**3,63 days**	**Wed 22/05/19**	**Mon 27/05/19**		
Set up environment in Azure	2 days	Wed 22/05/19	Thu 23/05/19		vendor,cust
Prepare project plan for SAP and get approval	2 hrs	Fri 24/05/19	Fri 24/05/19	2	consultant,cust
Plan GoingLive sessions	1 hr	Fri 24/05/19	Fri 24/05/19	3	
Get new SAP license agreement	1 day	Fri 24/05/19	Mon 27/05/19	4	cust
Order the migration kit	1 hr	Mon 27/05/19	Mon 27/05/19	5	cust
Order the installation package for new platform	1 hr	Mon 27/05/19	Mon 27/05/19	6	cust
Analyse SAP landscape	**3,25 days**	**Wed 22/05/19**	**Mon 27/05/19**		**consultant**
Database layout (tablespaces/db spaces)	1 day	Wed 22/05/19	Wed 22/05/19		
Configuration of ERP (distribution of dialog instances, batch…)	2 hrs	Thu 23/05/19	Thu 23/05/19	9	consultant,cust
CCMS configuration (operation modes, profiles …)	2 hrs	Thu 23/05/19	Thu 23/05/19	10	consultant,cust
Interfaces to other applications (RightFax, SAPComm …)	2 hrs	Thu 23/05/19	Thu 23/05/19	11	consultant,cust
Backup strategy	1 day	Thu 23/05/19	Fri 24/05/19	12	consultant,cust
Printer configuration	2 hrs	Fri 24/05/19	Fri 24/05/19	13	consultant,cust
Methods of data archiving	2 hrs	Mon 27/05/19	Mon 27/05/19	14	consultant,cust

Figure 7.1: Preparation phase

The plan includes all three phases discussed in this chapter—the preparation phase, the migration phase and the follow-up phase. The preparation phase is the easiest, as shown in Figure 7.1 (the screenshot contains European spelling, date format and number format). We analyze the current environment and gather the necessary information, people, and tools needed for the migration.

Task Name	Duration	Start	Finish	Predecessors	Resource Names
Migrations	**29 days**	**Fri 24/05/19**	**Wed 3/07/19**		
GoingLive - Migration Check	25,75 days	Mon 27/05/19	Tue 2/07/19	5	cust;SAP;consultant
Development	**25 days**	**Fri 24/05/19**	**Thu 27/06/19**		
Deploy system in Azure + OS	2 days	Fri 24/05/19	Mon 27/05/19	2	cust
Configure Disk Layout	2 days	Tue 28/05/19	Wed 29/05/19	19	cust
SAP Installation on target host	4 hrs	Thu 30/05/19	Thu 30/05/19	20	consultant
Test migration	3 days	Thu 30/05/19	Tue 4/06/19	21	consultant
Migration Post-Processing actions	2 hrs	Tue 4/06/19	Tue 4/06/19	22	consultant,cust
Adapt printer configuration	2 days	Tue 4/06/19	Thu 6/06/19	23	cust
Adapt external communication (ftp, rfc, archivlink)	3 days	Thu 6/06/19	Tue 11/06/19	24	cust
Set up SAP integration with Storage Manager	1 day	Tue 11/06/19	Wed 12/06/19	25	cust
Backup/recovery Tests	3 days	Wed 12/06/19	Mon 17/06/19	26	cust
ABAP developers testing	5 days	Mon 17/06/19	Mon 24/06/19	27	cust
Key-Users acceptance tests	5 days	Mon 17/06/19	Mon 24/06/19	27	cust
Final migration	2 days	Mon 24/06/19	Wed 26/06/19	28,29	consultant
Migration Post-Processing actions	2 hrs	Wed 26/06/19	Wed 26/06/19	30	consultant,cust
End-user support	1 day	Thu 27/06/19	Thu 27/06/19	31	consultant

Figure 7.2: The migrations

The different migrations are separated by system, as shown in Figure 7.2 and Figure 7.3 (the screenshots contain European date format and number format). This separation makes it easier to modify the project plan depending on the number of SAP landscapes and the number of SAP systems in each. The steps are more or less the same for each system.

Task Name	Duration	Start	Finish	Predecessors	Resource Names
Production	**29 days**	**Fri 24/05/19**	**Wed 3/07/19**		
Deploy system in Azure + OS	2 days	Fri 24/05/19	Mon 27/05/19	2	cust
Configure Disk Layout	2 days	Tue 28/05/19	Wed 29/05/19	49	cust
SAP Installation on target host	4 hrs	Thu 30/05/19	Thu 30/05/19	50	consultant
Test migration	3 days	Thu 30/05/19	Tue 4/06/19	51	consultant
Migration Post-Processing actions	2 hrs	Tue 4/06/19	Tue 4/06/19	52	consultant;cust
Configure SAP integration with High Availability software	1 day	Tue 4/06/19	Wed 5/06/19	53	consultant
High Availability Tests	3 days	Wed 5/06/19	Mon 10/06/19	54	
Adapt printer configuration	2 days	Mon 10/06/19	Wed 12/06/19	55	cust
Adapt external communication (ftp, rfc, archivlink)	3 days	Wed 12/06/19	Mon 17/06/19	56	cust
Set up SAP integration with Storage Manager	1 day	Mon 17/06/19	Tue 18/06/19	57	cust
Backup/recovery Tests	3 days	Tue 18/06/19	Fri 21/06/19	58	cust
ABAP developers testing	5 days	Fri 21/06/19	Fri 28/06/19	59	
Key-Users acceptance tests	5 days	Fri 21/06/19	Fri 28/06/19	59	cust
GoingLive - Migration Check	1 day	Fri 21/06/19	Mon 24/06/19	59	cust;SAP;consultant
Final migration	2 days	Fri 28/06/19	Tue 2/07/19	62;60;61	consultant
Migration Post-Processing actions	2 hrs	Tue 2/07/19	Tue 2/07/19	63	consultant;cust
End-user support	1 day	Wed 3/07/19	Wed 3/07/19	64	consultant
Follow-Up	**30 days**	**Thu 4/07/19**	**Wed 14/08/19**		
GoingLive - Migration Check - Production	1 day	Thu 4/07/19	Thu 4/07/19	65	cust;SAP;consultant
Keep old production system for reference	6 wks	Thu 4/07/19	Wed 14/08/19	65	

Figure 7.3: Migration of the production system and follow-up

The migration sequence is clearly defined in the project plan. Many customers want to use the migration opportunity to refresh all acceptance systems with a copy of the production systems. The acceptance systems are then re-installed using a copy of production, after the production migration. The project starts by copying the production system to the sandbox system and performing dry runs of the migrations on the sandbox system. When everything is verified, the development and production systems can be migrated. Finally, the acceptance systems are installed, using a copy of the already migrated production systems.

In this example, there are two migrations for the production systems. A test migration is followed by the live migration. For the other systems, one migration is carried out.

Every migration consists of the following steps:

- export on the source system
- SAP installation + database import
- post-migration activities
- set up management tools/monitoring
- set up backup and recovery test
- configure/migrate scripts related to the SAP system

You need to modify the time needed for each task based on progressive insight. Not only do your operating system and database change, or worse, both, a lot of tools also change. It is wise to factor in some extra time for the 'learning curve' and the unexpected.

7.3 Project team

A migration project should not be taken lightly, and a comprehensive team is needed to successfully complete the project.

The following section outlines the specific roles required for a migration project.

7.3.1 Your team

It is you, or more likely management, who makes the decision to migrate SAP to another platform. Even if you have no say and the decision comes crashing down on you from the executive level, you will still be responsible for successfully completing the project. Your first task will be to inform the relevant parties—SAP, software suppliers, consulting partners, system administrators, developers, and key users. Once the project gets started, you will have to make sure it keeps moving in the right direction and at the right speed.

This means that you will have to follow up the other parties' allocated tasks, mediate to resolve conflicts, and detect and find the right resources to fix technical and logistical problems.

Management

The managers of every department affected by the migration need to be aware of the process and must commit to its success. This is not so hard to achieve on the IT side, where the benefit, or at least the necessity, of the migration is most likely understood. However, it could be tougher to get the management of other departments on board. This is mainly because a platform migration, unlike an upgrade, does not bring new functionality. When presenting the project, you should emphasize the positive consequences in terms of future growth, system stability, improved support, potential for better performance, and total cost of ownership. But, make sure the short-term impacts (e.g., downtime and part-time involvement of test users) are also clearly understood.

Project manager

The project manager is responsible for managing the migration project.

Developers

ABAP code is portable between operating systems and databases. The applications delivered by SAP therefore run without any modification on the new platform. The same applies to programs developed in-house or by third parties, unless these programs contain platform-dependent code. Normally, no such code exists, but there are a few possible exceptions.

Developers must check non-SAP code for OS-dependent and DB-dependent program statements, and make an inventory of programs that must be modified. Unless the platform-dependent coding can be replaced with portable ABAP code, modifying the programs is only possible after migrating the sandbox system or development system.

Key users

By *key users*, we mean users with an extensive knowledge of the various business applications; these could be real end users, in-house application specialists, developers or consultants. A crucial task in every platform migration is the creation of a test suite of reports that are used to validate the data. These reports run in the source system before the migration, and also in the target system after the migration, and should produce identical results.

SAP administrators

SAP administrators should be involved at every stage. They need to work closely with the migration consultant. SAP administrators are responsible for configuring the backups, managing the output and, last but not least, adapting the interfaces to the new environment. A change in operating system and/or database implies training. This should be carried out at an early stage of the project.

7.3.2 Your consulting partner

Project manager

The project manager is responsible for managing migration projects. In large projects, and depending on the customer environment, the project manager could be provided by the consulting partner.

SAP architecture consultant

The principal SAP architecture consultant is responsible for designing the SAP environment. They should be highly experienced in both the source database and the target database, and the operating system platform. They assist you in designing the target SAP infrastructure, taking the new functionalities of the target platform into account, such as high availability, disaster recovery, etc.

Migration consultant

The migration consultant carries out the test and production migrations—the database is analyzed, data is unloaded or exported, SAP and the database software are installed on the target, data is loaded or imported into the target, and the standard post-processing actions are performed. They can also assist you in drawing up the project plan.

Migration consultants must have a special certification that allows them to perform OS/DB migrations. This certification is obtained through the SAP TADM70 training course. Note that you must secure the services of a certified migration consultant for the heterogeneous migration of any system, not just for the production system.

Almost all consulting companies that work with SAP (including SAP itself) have consultants with the required certification. When looking for a consultant, SAP or your usual partner are the obvious first stop, but you can also obtain a list of certified migration consultants from your local SAP support organization.

Performance and tuning consultant

The performance and tuning consultant is responsible for the performance and tuning of the SAP environment. They should be highly experienced in both the source database and the target database, as well as the operating system platform. They assist the ABAP developers to adapt their source code to the target database and operating system.

7.3.3 SAP

You must contact SAP and state your intention to migrate to a different platform as early as possible. If your company works directly with SAP, you should contact the contract administration department of your local SAP office, or you can go through your SAP account representative. If you do not deal with SAP directly, but via a partner, you must inform your partner first.

Ultimately, SAP must always be made aware of your migration project because your license must be amended; without a changed license you cannot obtain the installation kit for the new platform. If you plan to migrate a production system, you must order the OS/DB Migration Service.

8 1-2-3 Go!

In this chapter, we cover the three major activities of a platform migration—preparation, migration, and go-live and post migration.

8.1 Preparation phase

Depending on the size of the SAP landscape, the number of systems to be migrated, and the complexity of the environment, it is recommended to create a sandbox environment. The migrations can therefore be tested without impacting ongoing projects. As an alternative, acceptance and pre-production systems can be selected as source systems if a sandbox environment cannot be built.

8.1.1 Architecture design

You need to be well prepared before migrating your SAP landscape to the Cloud, and you need to spend adequate time on the architectural design and strategy. Don't forget that capacity planning, high availability and disaster recovery are implemented differently in the Cloud than on-premise.

A proper assessment of the current landscape and future requirements are key to a successful transition.

So, what do you need?

1. **Inventory of the current SAP components and applications**. You need to know how they are set up on-premise, the high-availability setup, and the disaster-recovery setup; if possible, with the number of SAPS and IOPS delivered by the current server and storage infrastructure. In addition, create an inventory of all SAP interfaces (SAP and non-SAP).

2. **Detailed database and SAP kernel and support package version for each SAP component**. Not all OS releases that are supported by SAP are also supported on Azure. The same is true for the database. An OS migration, database, and SAP kernel or support package up-

grade might be needed. You should consult the following SAP support notes and documentation:

- SAP Note 1928533—"SAP Applications on Azure: Supported Products and Azure VM types". This note defines the minimum OS releases supported in Azure VMs. It also defines the minimum database releases required for most non-HANA databases. The note also covers the sizing of the different SAP-supported Azure VM types.
- SAP Note 2039619—"SAP Applications on Microsoft Azure using the Oracle Database: Supported Products and Versions". This note defines the Oracle support matrix on Azure. Oracle only supports Windows and Oracle Linux as a guest OS in Azure for SAP workload. This support statement also applies to the SAP application layer running SAP instances.
- SAP Note 2235581—"SAP HANA: Supported Operating Systems". This provides the support matrix for SAP HANA on the different OS releases.
- SAP HANA-supported Azure VMs and HANA Large Instances are listed in the SAP-certified and supported SAP HANA Hardware Directory.
- The SAP Product Availability Matrix

3. **Decide which Azure Regions to deploy in.** The choice depends on the services available in the region and the distance to your on-premise installation.

4. **Network architecture to connect from on-premise to Azure, and the network topology within Azure**. Will you go for a Site-to-Site connection or ExpressRoute? You also need to consider the Active Directory and DNS design.

5. **The future layout of your SAP components in the Cloud**, complete with VM and storage layout. Sizing of compute, storage and networking components should be taken into account. We recommend three-tier designs for SAP production systems. By this, we mean separate VMs for the SCS, application servers and the database. This design guarantees the best flexibility with respect to high availability and disaster recovery.

6. **Business continuity and disaster-recovery architecture**. For high availability, check what the desired RDBMS has to offer. Most RDBMSs offer synchronous methods or a hot standby, which is recommended for production systems. For disaster recovery across different Azure Regions, most databases support asynchronous replication or log-shipping.

7. **Understand that not every application needs to be migrated to Azure**. In production environments in particular, it is advisable to keep applications such as SAP Console, used for barcode scanning, with end users. Ideally, the applications which remain on-premise will be connected to Azure using ExpressRoute.

8. **Verify your Microsoft Premier Support Contract**. This is a support requirement set out by SAP. For support requirements by SAP, refer to SAP Note 2015553—"SAP on Microsoft Azure: Support Prerequisites".

8.1.2 Migration methodology

There are different methods to move an SAP system from on-premise to the Azure Cloud:

1. The most straightforward method is to move your virtual machines by uploading the VHD which contains the OS, the SAP binaries and the database installation, plus the VHD which contains the database data and log files. The host name and SAP SID remain the same. This option is only valid if you are already using Hyper-V. The disadvantage of this option is that the operating system, SAP version and database have to be supported on Azure. It is also not possible to adapt the installation to the best-practices applicable to a cloud installation.

2. Another option is backup/restore. A new SAP landscape is deployed, SAP and RDBMS are installed, and the database backup is restored. Most database vendors allow you to adapt the storage layout and restore in a higher database release than the source.

3. Last but not least, there is the export/import option, which we consider to be the most effective option. As with option 2, a new SAP landscape is deployed, and SAP and RDBMS are installed. The import

can be done to an operating system and database which differ from the source. Database compression and encryption can be enabled in the same step. To reduce downtime, export and import can run at the same time.

Multiple migration scenarios are outlined in the following sections. The scenario you end up using will be specific to your environment and will be outlined by your project manager during project execution. We now outline the various actions that you can take, depending on the different scenarios.

Copy production environment to a sandbox environment

By creating a copy of the current production environment on a sandbox environment, the migration can be tested without impacting ongoing projects. Migrations can be executed until successful, without needing to agree to downtime with the other parties involved. This is the same as if the migrations were done using existing test or quality assurance systems.

What are we copying?

When we refer to copying the production environment, we mean taking a copy of every production system: SAP ERP, BW, and CRM.

The SAP installations and system copies can be done using SAP's standard homogeneous system copy procedure. The standard technical post-processing actions, which are performed after a system copy, should be sufficient. Renaming the logical system names, which is normally time-consuming, is not necessary because the environment is isolated from the other SAP environments. It is, however, vital that the systems in the sandbox environment are correctly interconnected. This ensures that no sandbox system attempts to contact any real production system (see Figure 8.1).

It is, however, important to run the sandbox environment on a hardware infrastructure that is comparable to the production environment. This enables you to estimate the duration of the export and, subsequently, the duration of the migration. The hardware infrastructure does not need to be exactly the same because projections are possible.

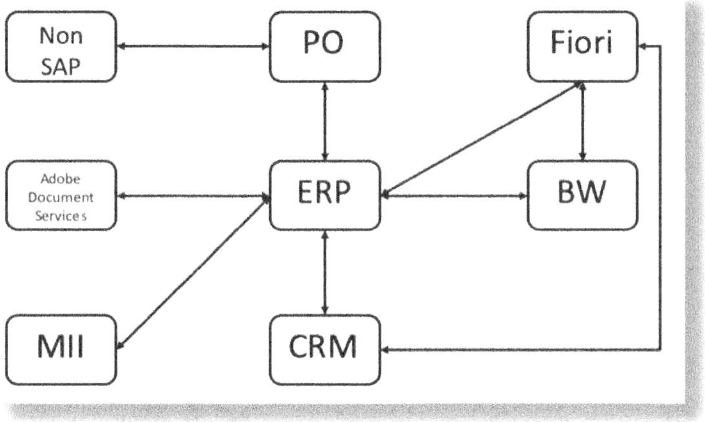

Figure 8.1: Sandbox systems interconnected

Using the existing acceptance or pre-production systems

If using a sandbox environment is not possible due to resource constraints, acceptance or pre-production systems can be used as source systems instead. This means downtime on these environments during the migration test runs. Because many projects take place simultaneously, agreeing and scheduling downtime among the different project teams might be an issue, especially because migrations might need to be executed several times.

The acceptance and pre-production systems must be from the same SAP release and support package level. The size of the database must be comparable so that the migration test is as representative of the production migration as possible.

For SAP landscapes that have no acceptance system or pre-production system, development systems can be used. Development systems are normally much smaller, and estimating the duration of the migration might not be so accurate. Development systems also tend to contain "leftovers" from previous development projects which never went into production, which were never finished, or which contain defects. These leftover issues might create too much of a diversion, because they will not occur in production.

8.2 Migration phase

A migration project consists of different migration phases: pilot migrations, technical and functional testing, and migration of the production systems.

8.2.1 Pilot migrations

In the pilot (test) migrations, the first systems are migrated to the Cloud. Most customers start with copies of their production systems or test systems. In this phase, the assumptions made in the architecture design need to be verified. High-availability and disaster-recovery solutions need to be set up and validated. Performance and scalability tests are also advisable. Do not be disappointed if, after the test migrations, it is concluded that some parts of the architecture design need to be redone. Going back and forth is part of the game.

There are several points to consider and review during your pilot migrations:

- SAP data needs to be migrated from an on-premise system to the Cloud, whether via backup/restore or export/import. The network latency between your on-premise system and the Azure system is therefore a determining factor when it comes to downtime. You need to plan enough time to optimize the data transfer.
- Heterogeneous platform migrations, migrations in which the database or operating system changes, are done via export/import, using the migration tools from SAP. Enough time should be planned to optimize these phases. An advantage of export/import is that both steps can be run at the same time. As soon as a table, or part of a table, is exported, it is transferred to the target system and imported straight away. We have seen cases in which export/import was faster than backup/restore because the former can be done in parallel, but the latter is sequential. Using export/import for a homogeneous migration makes sense. Next to the parallelization of activities, data can be imported in a higher database release, combining the migration with a database upgrade.
- After the migration, validate the VM types and storage. Does the selected infrastructure match expectations? If not, a re-alignment might be needed. For example, it is recommended to enable database compression during the migration to Azure. You need to use the export/import methodology to do so. Database compression has a positive impact on I/O performance because less data needs to be read from the disks. Data is decompressed using CPU resources before it is transferred to the application. The performance impact on the CPU is, however, negligible and does not outweigh the positive impact on I/O performance. By enabling database compression, you might end up with a much smaller database than you had on-premise. Figures of 50% to 80% are common. When compression is activated during the migration, a review after the pilot migration of your storage layout might be needed.
- Include sufficient time to set up high-availability and disaster-recovery procedures. Although the concepts are comparable to on-premise installations, the implementation is not. Keep in mind that you need to use load balancers, Windows or Linux Failover Clusters across availability sets or zones.

In the next step, a copy of every production system is migrated to the new infrastructure. Issues encountered during the migration must be documented. For every migrated system, an initial performance and tuning session must also be planned and completed.

All systems need to be interconnected as soon as they are all available on the target platform. The interconnection of all the systems is a vital prerequisite for technical and functional acceptance testing, which is carried out in a later step.

The migration consultant carries out the migrations—the database is analyzed, data is unloaded, SAP and the database software are installed on the target, data is loaded into the target, and the standard post-processing actions are performed. The SAP administrator must also be involved in the migrations. They work closely together with the migration consultant in order to familiarize themselves with the target environment.

8.2.2 Technical and functional testing

This is a critical phase of the migration project, which requires extensive involvement of your resources (administrators, developers, application specialists and key users). All the newly installed systems need to be adapted to the new platform and rigorously tested. Many people from different organizations need to be involved in these tests and should approve or reject the new environment before it goes live.

For the individual systems, you are responsible for executing the following tasks:

- High-availability configuration, setup and testing—the integration between SAP, the database and the high-availability software needs to be set up and thoroughly tested. Test your high-availability and disaster-recovery procedures. Simulate failover situations by shutting down VMs. Measure the time needed to failover. If it takes too long, improvements to the setup or solution will be needed.
- Operating system, database and SAP backup configuration and recovery testing—the integration between the backup software and the database needs to be configured. A recovery test with roll-

forward is a necessity. Make sure that the time needed for recovery meets RTO and RPO requirements.

- Disaster-recovery exercises—the failover to the secondary data center needs to be tested and documented.
- If a monitoring infrastructure is in place, integration between the new environment and the monitoring system needs to be established.
- Output management needs to be set up and configured. Key users should be able to test the printing mechanism on the new environment, especially if barcode printing is in place.
- Detect and adapt ABAP-dependent database and operating-system-dependent code. Sufficient time should be allocated to this task if both the operating system and database change. Customer ABAP code needs to be verified for database-dependent SQL commands (using EXEC SQL). Don't forget that your custom code needs to be SAP HANA-compliant if the target database is SAP HANA. If the operating system changes, all calls to external commands or programs, as well as access to operating system files and directories, should be verified.
- Interfaces need to be tested and adapted. This step should not be underestimated if both the operating system and database change. Because interfaces are in most cases system and customer-specific, it is necessary to have input and cooperation from the SAP administrator, developers and key users.
- Cross-system business processes need to be tested. Business consultants and key users are required for this.
- Close attention must be given to the performance of the systems. They must be adapted while tests continue in order to reach an optimal configuration before live migration. At a minimum, you should:
    - compare the top 10 dialog transactions to the current SAP installation,
    - compare the top 10 batch jobs to the current SAP installation, and
    - compare data transfers through the interfaces to and from the SAP system. Don't forget that data might need to be transferred between the Cloud and the systems still installed on-premise.

8.2.3 The real migration

In the following section, we cover several migration scenarios. The project manager and the stakeholders select the chosen scenario at the beginning of the project. The following paragraphs outline the actions that you should take, depending on the scenario chosen.

Scenario 1: Vertical migrations

In a vertical migration project, migration of the development, acceptance and production systems in the SAP landscape are done at the same time, or one after the other in a short time frame (see Figure 8.2).

This approach has the following advantages:

- There is no mixed environment, or only a short-term mixed environment.
- There is no development freeze, or only a short-term development freeze.
- There is no need for an external tool to mount the transport file system between the environments.

SAP develops software, keeping operating system and database independency in mind. Transporting changes between systems running on different platforms is supported as long as you do not include any operating system or database-dependent code. This is already the case with SAP standard software.

To avoid issues, or to avoid the constant filtering of transport requests to verify what is inside, we advise a development freeze. In a vertical migration project, the freeze period is limited because the migrations are done in a short time frame.

The disadvantage of this approach is that because all systems are migrated one after the other, within a short time, there is little room for testing; problems might go undetected, only to be found in production.

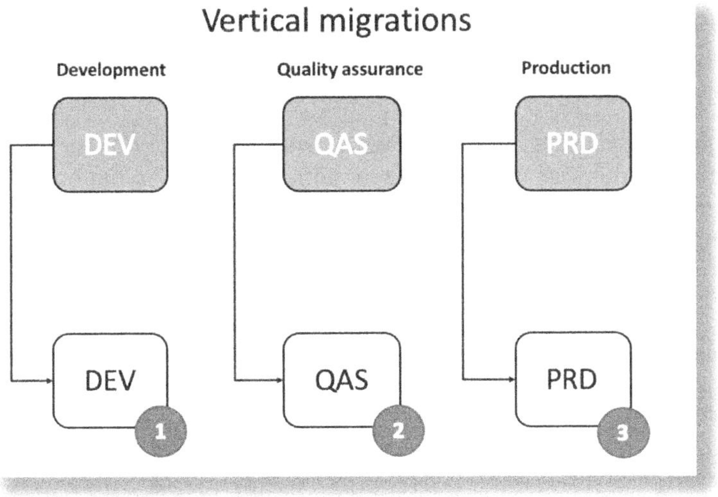

Figure 8.2: Vertical SAP migrations

Scenario 2: Horizontal migrations

The days of a standalone SAP ERP system are long gone. These days, many customers run SAP ERP, SCM, BW, and many more. Many of these systems are interconnected due to cross-system business processes. We therefore strongly recommend combining systems in groups, and migrating them together. If possible, all interconnected systems should be migrated over one weekend.

The advantages of combining systems are:

- Systems with strong interconnection, such as SAP ERP, BW, and CRM are migrated at the same time (see Figure 8.3). For example, CRM cannot function without ERP due to cross-system business processes, so migrating them over different weekends makes no sense. CRM functionality without a running ERP system is not available anyway.
- SAP ERP and BW transfer huge amounts of data. Migrating them at the same time is strongly recommended when the systems need to be moved to a new data center. In this way, the systems go

down together and wake up again together, in the new data center, just as they were in the old one. This avoids having to send huge amounts of data over a WAN connection when migrations are done separately.

- Migrating systems in groups has a positive impact on the project plan. The number of weekends is limited to several big-bang migration weekends. This reduces downtime for the business and limits weekend work for everyone involved in the migration project.

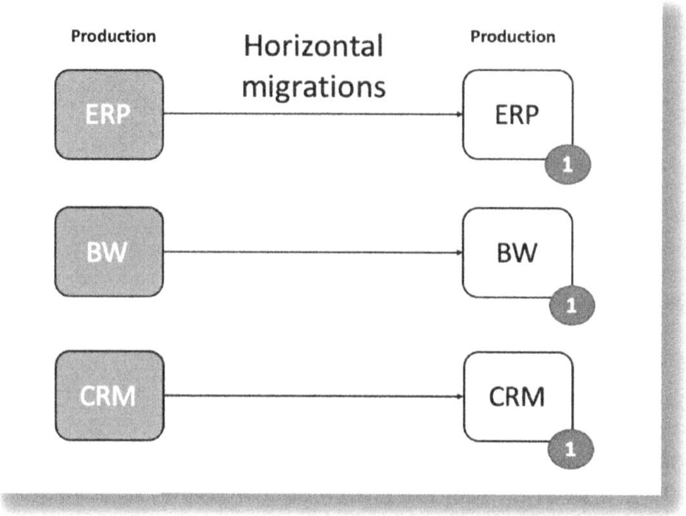

Figure 8.3: Horizontal migrations

You need to determine whether a horizontal migration is a feasible and acceptable approach, and the decision depends on many things, such as:

- Migrating several systems at once means that more than one system is unavailable at a given time. Is this acceptable for the business? The impact of migrating one system at a time might be far lower than when migrating a group of systems at once; business processes not using the migrating system remain available and continue to function.
- Exporting, transferring and importing several systems at once has a huge impact on the infrastructure. Is I/O throughput and network bandwidth capable of coping with such a load? This could create a

bottleneck, especially on the source environment which is running on older hardware.

- Several migration consultants, system administrators and key users need to be available during these big-bang weekends. Careful planning is needed.
- Making more than one system live at once impacts the helpdesk. This should not be underestimated. For example, you can expect a lot of calls from users who did not get the latest version of the SAPLOGON.INI.

Scenario 3: Combination of vertical and horizontal migrations

The final scenario is a combination of the first two scenarios. Systems that communicate frequently are migrated at the same time (horizontal migrations). These combinations of systems are extended to the development and acceptance systems of those landscapes (vertical migrations).

From a project perspective, several landscapes are dealt with at the same time.

Recommendation

Based on our migration project experience, we strongly recommend using the second scenario—horizontal migrations. Our reasoning is as follows:

- SAP ERP and CRM cannot function without each other due to cross-system business processes. Most of the CRM transactional data resides in the ERP system. Migrating them over different weekends makes no sense. CRM functionality without a running ERP system is not available anyway.
- SAP BW extracts huge amounts of data from the ERP system. A migration to the Cloud is a migration to another data center. Keeping your BW system in a separate data center to your ERP results in a large amount of data to be sent over the WAN. It is therefore recommended to migrated them on the same weekend.

8.2.4 Go-live and post-production phase

During the live migration, make sure that you follow the checklist that you developed earlier. Execute the steps one by one and make sure that the outcome is the same as during the test migrations. Any last-minute changes in the conversion plan should be made with caution.

The following steps should be considered at the production system's go-live stage:

1. After migration, make sure that your business owners execute all validated test scenarios as previously agreed. It is important to validate data consistency by running the business reports. The results in the target system should be the same as the results in the source system.
2. Reconnect all interfaces to SAP and non-SAP applications and verify that they function correctly.
3. Reconfigure the transport system and execute a transport.
4. Execute a database backup before releasing the system for production. In addition, perform a VM backup of the SAP Application Servers. Note that as soon as the system is released, there is no turning back.

5. Make sure that the non-migrated system can still communicate with the migrated system. You might need to reset the host name buffer in SAP to do so. This step gets rid of the old cached IP addresses associated with the names of the application instances you moved into the Cloud.

Your migration consultant, the SAP administrators and your key users must be on-site at go-live because you can expect many end user calls in the days following the migration of the production system.

Be ready for the following issues to arise:

- Users are unable to connect to the new system because their SAP Logon was not adapted.
- Users are unable to print because the connection to some print servers was not correctly adapted.
- Background jobs are aborted because some ABAP programs slipped through the test phases and still contain OS-specific or DB-specific statements.

After the production system migration, there will be one more verification session by SAP. This normally occurs three to four weeks after the live migration and will have been taken into account in the project plan and cost.

For every production system, you should also perform detailed performance analyses one or two weeks after the system goes into production, and again one month later. Each performance analysis should provide you with a detailed performance and tuning audit, including your ABAP code, which has the most impact on system performance.

If your migration went smoothly and the environment has stabilized, the focus is then on monitoring, operating, and administering the system. From an SAP perspective, you perform the same tasks that you were required to perform before the migration.

It might be a good idea to review your environment after it has run for a few weeks in production. Although preparation is everything, it is difficult to estimate sizing requirements beforehand. Virtual machines might need to be upscaled, downscaled or shut down.

9 Customer example

In this chapter, we describe a customer that migrated their SAP environment to the Azure Cloud. We discuss the business case and describe how they mapped their current infrastructure to the Cloud, taking the Azure capabilities into account, and how they implemented high availability and disaster recovery.

Our reference customer ran SAP in a 24/7 production environment. The application was considered business critical. The Recovery Point Objective (RPO) was set at five minutes, the Recovery Time Objective (RTO) was less strict, and was at a maximum of four hours.

▶ **Why go for the Cloud?**

The on-premise infrastructure was reaching its limit and was no longer supported by the hardware vendor. Even more critical, their data center infrastructure no longer complied with today's standards. Last but not least, there was a business requirement for a secondary data center at least 30 miles away from the first. The TCO calculation quickly revealed that replacing the infrastructure (systems, storage and network), modernizing the data center, and building or renting a secondary data center were far too expensive and made no sense.

▶ **The source environment**

The SAP landscape consisted of the following components (see Figure 9.1):

- SAP ERP—run on SAP ASE or Sybase. The operating system was AIX, with IBM POWER as the underlying hardware infrastructure. The SAP ERP landscape consisted of development, acceptance and production systems.
- SAP BW—also run on SAP ASE or Sybase. Also installed on AIX, with IBM POWER as the underlying infrastructure. As with SAP ERP, the BW landscape consisted of development, acceptance and production systems.

- SAP Business Objects—run on Windows with SQL Server on VMware. There was only a development system and a production system.
- SAP MII (Manufacturing, Intelligence and Integration)—run on Windows with SQL Server on VMWare. SAP MII was delocalized and installed in the different production plants. There were three SAP MII landscapes, consisting of a development system and a production system.
- Solution Manager—run on SAP ASE, AIX on IBM POWER. There was only a production system.

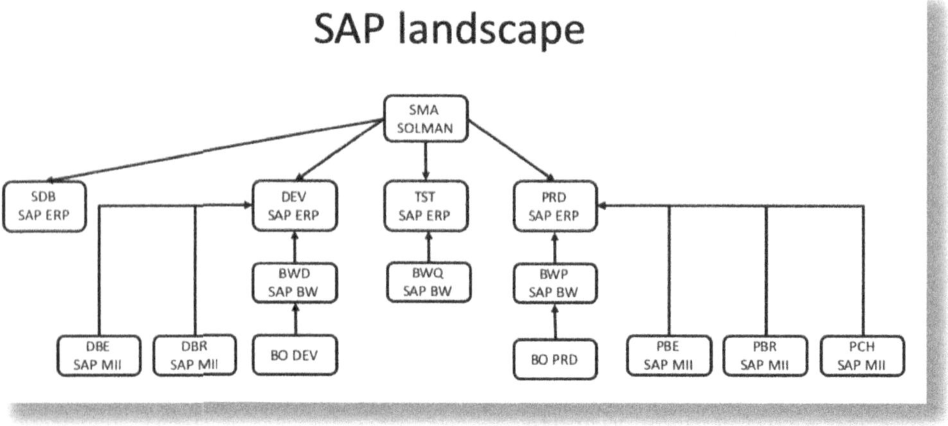

Figure 9.1: The SAP landscape

SAP ERP, BW, Business Objects and Solution Manager were installed in the European data center. The SAP MII systems were delocalized and installed on-premise in the production plants in Europe, Latin America and China. The MII systems connected over the Internet to the backend SAP ERP system.

9.1 The on-premise environment

Step one of our architecture design was to create an inventory of the customer's current environment and to map it to Azure capabilities. We needed to consider the layout of the SAP components, number of application servers, high availability and disaster recovery. We estimated the number of SAPS of the current environment by using the hardware documentation from the hardware vendor. In situations where you are unable to determine the maximum number of SAPS the current infrastructure is capable of delivering, use the number of CPUs and memory instead and map those to the VM series offered in Azure and supported by SAP.

SAP-Landscape											
SID	SAP module	SAP version	Layout	System layout	CPU type and model	No of CPUs DB	No of CPUs app servers	RAM (GB) DB server	SAPS DB layer	SAPS app layer	SAPS Total
SBX	ERP	EHP7	CI+DB	2-tier	IBM Power7	2	0	48	6420	0	6420
DEV	ERP	EHP7	CI+DB	2-tier	IBM Power7	1	0	48	3210	0	3210
TST	ERP	EHP7	CI+DB	2-tier	IBM Power7	1	0	56	3210	0	3210
PRD	ERP	EHP7	CI+DB	3-tier	IBM Power7	7	4	72	22470	12840	35310
PRD	ERP	EHP7	DB (standby)	3-tier	IBM Power7	2	4	72	22470	12840	35310
PRD	ERP	EHP7	AS	3-tier	IBM Power7	0	2	48	9630	0	9630
PRD	ERP	EHP7	AS	3-tier	IBM Power7	0	2	48	9630	0	9630
BWD	BW	7.40	CI+DB	2-tier	IBM Power7	1	0	48	3210	0	3210
BWQ	BW	7.40	CI+DB	2-tier	IBM Power7	3	0	48	9630	0	9630
BWP	BW	7.40	CI+DB	2-tier	IBM Power7	4	0	72	12840	0	12840
SMA	SolMan	7.1	CI+DB	2-tier	IBM Power7	1	0	16	3210	0	3210
DBE	MII	7.40	CI+DB	2-tier	Intel	2	0	8	4564	0	4564
PBE	MII	7.40	CI+DB	2-tier	Intel	2	0	16	4564	0	4564
DBR	MII	7.40	CI+DB	2-tier	Intel	2	0	8	4564	0	4564
PBR	MII	7.40	CI+DB	2-tier	Intel	1	0	4	2282	0	2282
PCH	MII	7.40	CI+DB	2-tier	Intel	1	0	4	2282	0	2282

Table 9.1: On-premise SAP layout

Table 9.1 lists the current SAP systems with the hardware resources used, the amount of memory, number of CPUs and, most importantly, the number of SAPS the current infrastructure is capable of delivering.

SAP Landscape		Source Software			
SID	SAP Module	OS type	OS version	DB vendor & Version	DB version
SBX	ERP	AIX	7.1	SAP ASE	ASE 15
DEV	ERP	AIX	7.1	SAP ASE	ASE 15
TST	ERP	AIX	7.1	SAP ASE	ASE 15
PRD	ERP	AIX	7.1	SAP ASE	ASE 15
PRD	ERP	AIX	7.1	SAP ASE	ASE 15
PRD	ERP	AIX	7.1	SAP ASE	ASE 15
PRD	ERP	AIX	7.1	SAP ASE	ASE 15
BWD	BW	AIX	7.1	SAP ASE	ASE 15
BWQ	BW	AIX	7.1	SAP ASE	ASE 15
BWP	BW	AIX	7.1	SAP ASE	ASE 15
SMA	SolMan	AIX	7.1	SAP ASE	ASE 15
DBE	MII	WINDOWS	2012 R2	MSSQL	2012
PBE	MII	WINDOWS	2012 R2	MSSQL	2012
DBR	MII	WINDOWS	2012 R2	MSSQL	2012
PBR	MII	WINDOWS	2012 R2	MSSQL	2012
PCH	MII	WINDOWS	2012 R2	MSSQL	2012

Table 9.2: SAP components, OS and DB versions

We have also created an inventory of the current operating system and database vendors and versions (see Table 9.2). This information is important in order to verify whether the current operating system and/or database is supported on Azure, or if an operating system or database migration is needed.

In our customer's case, AIX was not supported on Azure and SAP ASE did not meet the minimum requirements to be supported on Azure. SAP ASE is only supported on Azure as of version 16. An OS/DB migration was therefore the only option. Fortunately, the advantage of using the OS/DB procedure, or export/import, is that we could import in a higher release of ASE, thereby avoiding a database upgrade altogether.

The MII systems use Windows 2012 and SQL Server 2012, which are supported on Azure. As we were moving to new hardware anyway, we took the opportunity to re-deploy the MII systems on Windows 2016 and SQL Server 2016, so we used export/import for the MII systems as well.

Last but not least, we needed information about the existing storage layout, data replication requirements, SLA agreements and operation mode expectation (see Table 9.3).

SAP Landscape		Storage			SLA's	
SID	SAP Module	DB Size (GB)	Two DC concept	Data replication	SLA (Availability)	Operation mode
SBX	ERP	1450	No	No	99.9	5*8
DEV	ERP	900	Yes	Yes	99.9	5*8
TST	ERP	1050	No	No	99.9	5*8
PRD	ERP	1450	Yes	Yes	99.9	7*24
PRD	ERP	0	No	No	99.9	7*24
PRD	ERP	0	No	No	99.9	7*24
PRD	ERP	0	No	No	99.9	7*24
BWD	BW	600	Yes	Yes	99.9	7*24
BWQ	BW	1250	Yes	Yes	99.9	7*24
BWP	BW	1850	Yes	Yes	99.9	7*24
SMA	Solution Manager	125	Yes	Yes	99.9	5*8
DBE	MII	6	Yes	Yes	99.9	5*8
PBE	MII	15	Yes	Yes	99.9	7*24
DBR	MII	6	No	No	99.9	5*8
PBR	MII	15	No	No	99.9	7*24
PCH	MII	15	No	No	99.9	7*24

Table 9.3: High availability and storage layout

9.2 Architecture design

There are three steps involved in designing architecture, which we also followed in our customer's case. First, we selected the virtual machines, then we defined the storage layout. Finally, we designed the high-availability and disaster-recovery scenarios.

9.2.1 Selecting the virtual machines

SID	CPU type and model	No of CPUs	RAM (GB) DB Server	RAM (GB) App Servers	SAPS DB Layer	SAPS App layer	SAPS Total	Azure VM	SAPS
SBX	IBM Power7	2	48		6420	0	6420	DS13v2 (8vCPU, 56 GB mem)	12300
DEV	IBM Power7	1	48		3210	0	3210	DS13v2 (8vCPU, 56 GB mem)	12300
TST	IBM Power7	1	56		3210	0	3210	DS13v2 (8vCPU, 56 GB mem)	12300
PRD	IBM Power7	7	72	48	22470	12,840	35310	DS14v2 (16 vCPU, 112 GB mem)	24180
PRD	IBM Power7	2	4	72	22470	12,840	35310	DS14v2 (16 vCPU, 112 GB mem)	24180
PRD	IBM Power7	0	2	48	9630	0	9630	DS13v2 (8vCPU, 56 GB mem)	12300
PRD	IBM Power7	0	2	48	9630	0	9630	DS13v2 (8vCPU, 56 GB mem)	12300
BWD	IBM Power7	1	48		3210	0	3210	DS13v2 (8vCPU, 56 GB mem)	12300
BWQ	IBM Power7	2,5	48		8025	0	8025	DS13v2 (8vCPU, 56 GB mem)	12300
BWP	IBM Power7	4	72		12840	0	12840	DS14v2 (16 vCPU, 112 GB mem)	24180
SMA	IBM Power7	1	16		3210	0	3210	DS12v2 (4vCPU, 28 GB mem)	6680
DBE	Intel	2	8		4564	0	4564	DS12v2 (4vCPU, 28 GB mem)	6680
PBE	Intel	2	16		4564	0	4564	DS12v2 (4vCPU, 28 GB mem)	6680
DBR	Intel	2	8		4564	0	4564	DS12v2 (4vCPU, 28 GB mem)	6680
PBR	Intel	1	4		2282	0	2282	DS11v2 (2vCPU, 14 GB mem)	3530
PCH	Intel	1	4		2282	0	2282	DS11v2 (2vCPU, 14 GB mem)	3530

Table 9.4: Matching the SAP components to VMs

As shown in Table 9.4, we matched the existing SAP layout to the virtual machines available in Azure, based on SAP Note 1928533—"SAP Applications on Azure: Supported Products and Azure VM types". In our customer example, we needed to consider the number of CPUs, memory, and SAPS each VM was capable of delivering.

9.2.2 Defining the storage layout

In the next step, we defined the storage layout. SAP systems read and write huge amounts of data, in and out of the database and most performance issues are caused by a lack of storage performance or I/O latency (see Table 9.5). This step was therefore extremely important for our customer. Our plan was as follows:

- As recommended by SAP, we used managed disks. In doing so, there was no need to distribute storage among different storage accounts to avoid the maximum number of IOPS set on those accounts. The additional advantage of managed disks was that availability sets were taken into account by default.
- In addition, we used premium (SSD) disks for the database data and log files. A stripe set for the datafiles was used to increase the number of IOPS.

		On-Premise			Azure			Disks Number	Storage	IOPS
BWP	C:	OS	100GB	**BWP**	C:	OS	100	1	P20: 512GB (managed OS)	2500
	D:	PAGEFILE	200GB	ASCS + AS + DB	D:	PAGEFILE	200	1	P20: 512GB (managed OS)	2500
8CPU /128GB	E:	SAPEXE	50GB	DS14v2 (16 vCPU, 112 GB mem)	E:	SAPEXE +TRANS	100	1	P20: 512GB (managed OS)	2500
	F:	SAPDATA	1TB		F:	SAPDATA	2000	2	P40: 2TB	7500
	G:	SAPDATA	2TB			SAPDATA	2000	3	P40: 2TB	7500
	H:	SAPDATA	1TB			SAPDATA	2000	4	P40: 2TB	7500
	I:	SAPDATA	1TB			DELETE				
	J:	SAPLOG	300GB		J:	SAPLOG	512	5	P20: 512GB	2500
	T:	SAPTRANS	50GB			DELETE				
ERP	C:	OS	100GB	**ERP**	C:	OS	100	1	P20: 512GB (managed OS)	2500
	D:	PAGEFILE	200GB	ASCS + DB	D:	PAGEFILE	200	1	P20: 512GB (managed OS)	2500
16CPU /128GB	E:	SAPEXE	50GB	DS14v2 (16 vCPU, 112 GB mem)	E:	SAPEXE +TRANS	100	1	P20: 512GB (managed OS)	2500
	F:	SAPDATA	1TB		F:	SAPDATA	2000	2	P40: 2TB	7500
	G:	SAPDATA	2TB			SAPDATA	2000	3	P40: 2TB	7500
	H:	SAPLOG	256GB		H:	SAPLOG	512	4	P20: 512GB	2500
	T:	SAPTRANS	50GB			DELETE				
ERP	C:	OS	100GB	**ERP**	C:	OS	100	1	P20: 512GB (managed OS)	2500
	D:	PAGEFILE	100GB	SAP Application Server	D:	PAGEFILE	200	1	P20: 512GB (managed OS)	2500
4CPU /64GB	E:	SAPEXE	50GB	DS13v2 (8vCPU, 56 GB mem)	E:	SAPEXE	100	1	P20: 512GB (managed OS)	2500
ERP	C:	OS	100GB	**ERP**	C:	OS	100	1	P20: 512GB (managed OS)	2500
	D:	PAGEFILE	100GB	SAP Application Server	D:	PAGEFILE	200	1	P20: 512GB (managed OS)	2500
4CPU /64GB	E:	SAPEXE	50GB	DS13v2 (8vCPU, 56 GB mem)	E:	SAPEXE	100	1	P20: 512GB (managed OS)	2500

Table 9.5: Storage layout

9.2.3 Designing the high-availability and disaster-recovery scenarios

The next step in our architecture design was to explore environment options which met the Azure requirements to achieve 99.9%, 99.95%, or 99.99% SLA uptime.

Microsoft guarantees the following SLA's for virtual machines deployed in Azure:

- For all single-instance virtual machines using premium storage for all operating system disks and data disks, Microsoft guarantees virtual machine connectivity of at least 99.9%.
- For all virtual machines that have two or more instances deployed in the same availability set, Microsoft guarantees virtual machine connectivity to at least one instance of at least 99.95%.
- For all virtual machines that have two or more instances deployed across two or more availability zones in the same Azure Region, Microsoft guarantees virtual machine connectivity to at least one instance of at least 99.99%.
- The 99.99% availability can be increased further by installing a fallback SAP environment in another region. Azure Site Recovery can be used to keep an updated copy of the virtual machines in the secondary region, while database mirroring or replication can be used to keep the SAP data synchronized.

The higher the availability SLA, the higher the TCO. The next step in our architectural plan was to create an infrastructure design for all three options—99.9%, 99.95% and 99.99%. This enabled us to compare availability against flexibility, complexity and TCO, and then decide which one to go with. Our possible architectural design options are outlined below.

For 99.9% availability:

An availability of 99.9% is guaranteed when you use premium storage. The system layout in this setup is very straightforward (see Figure 9.2). In our customer case, this meant:

- Three virtual machines for the SAP ERP system:
  - one VM for the Central Services Instance and database server (an SCS instance does not need many resources). We therefore planned to install it together with the database server. This avoided the need for a VM and operating system license which would have been the case if we had deployed the SCS instance on a dedicated VM.
  - two SAP Application Servers, each on their own virtual machine—there were two application servers in the on-premise installation. Keeping the same layout was the most straightforward option.
- One large virtual machine for the productive BW system—we could install the Central Service Instance, one SAP Application Server, and the database server on the same system. This was again a copy of the on-premise installation.
- A one-to-one mapping of the non-production systems to Azure—every non-production system was to be deployed on a dedicated VM with more or less the same capacity as the on-premise counterpart.

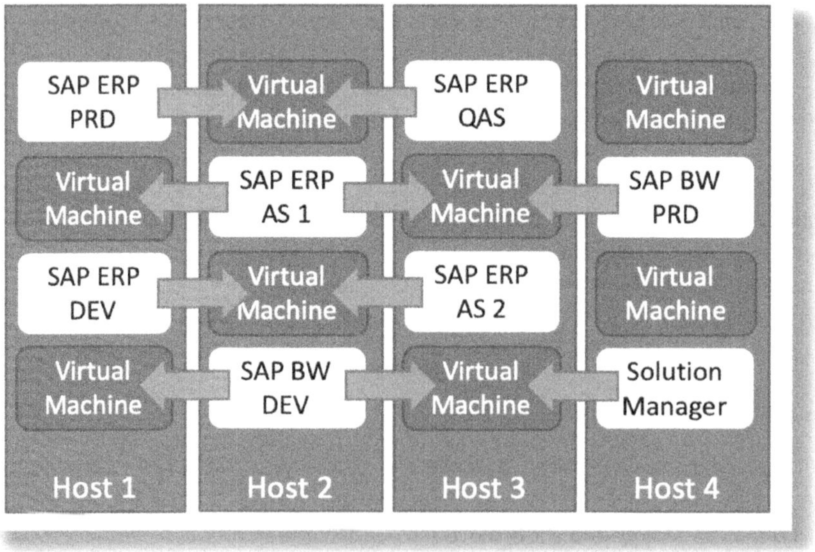

Figure 9.2: Availability on Azure, SLA 99.9%

For 99.95% availability

The next level was 99.95%. For this, we planned to use premium storage, as we did in the previous level. Additionally, we needed to assign systems to availability sets.

The system layout was as follows (see Figure 9.3):

- An availability set for the SAP Central Services component, which consisted of two virtual machines—the SCS component run on the primary VM and an ERS run on the secondary VM. The ERS could maintain a copy of the enqueue table in memory. If the primary VM failed, the SCS component would be failed over to the secondary on VM and then find a copy of the enqueue table. Both VMs were to be in a Windows cluster. The SIOS DataKeeper was needed in order to synchronize the global directory between both VMs. Finally, an Azure Load Balancer would be set in front of both VMs to direct incoming requests to the active VM.
- An availability set for the SAP Application Servers—we needed at least two. A load balancer was not needed because the message server component of the SCS could balance incoming requests to the best performing application server or, in case of unavailability, to the remaining application server. The Autostart parameter for the SAP Application Server would be enabled to make sure that the AS restarted when the VM did.
- An availability set for the database server—the database server would be protected using database technology, in this case Sybase Replication Server. SAP ASE provides a warm standby solution to transfer database changes from the primary to the secondary database. The installation and operation of SRS works in the same way on Azure as it does on-premise. SAP ASE HADR does not require an Azure Internal Load Balancer and has no dependencies on OS level clustering.

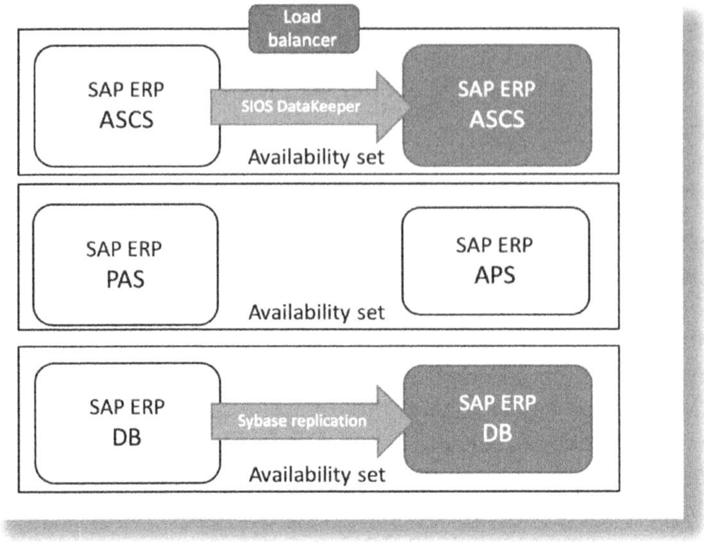

Figure 9.3: Availability on Azure, SLA 99.95%

For 99.99% availability

For 99.99% availability, we needed to extend our setup with availability zones. The technical setup with availability zones is comparable to the setup with availability sets (see Figure 9.4).

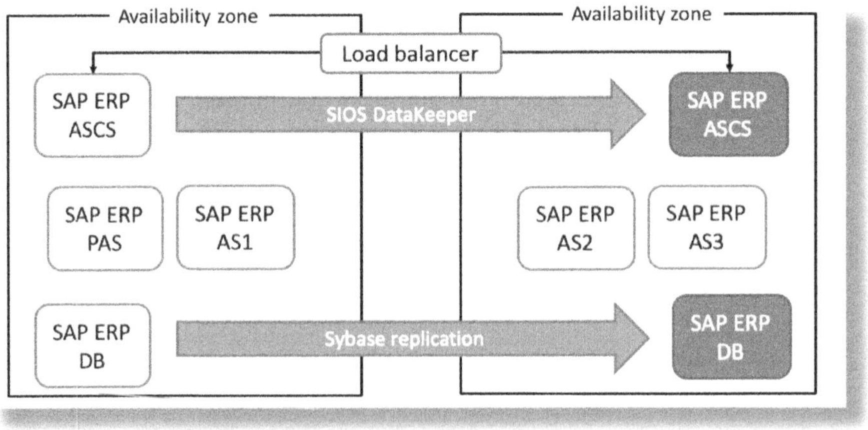

Figure 9.4: Availability on Azure, SLA 99.99%

There would be no additional cost to deploy virtual machines in availability zones. There would, however, be an additional cost for the data transfer between the VMs residing in different zones. In our customer's case, we calculated a transfer of 10GB of transaction data from the primary to the secondary database, per month. The cost for data transfer was negligible.

Availability could be further improved by using paired regions and maintaining a standby environment in the secondary region.

The layout would have looked as follows:

- A copy or image of all the virtual machines which reside in the primary region should be available in the secondary region. The SAP Central Services Instance and the SAP Application Servers would be static. The SAP repository, customizing and business data would reside in the database, so a one-time copy or image should be sufficient. What about the global directory? The global directory contains important files such as instance configuration, logfiles from background jobs, and much more. We could have used the SIOS DataKeeper to sync the global directory to the secondary virtual machine in the secondary region. However, we considered this overkill. We would only failover to the secondary region during a major disaster. The logs of the background jobs not being available was acceptable in an emergency.
- An operational virtual machine for the standby database server should be available in the secondary region. Because we would use database technology for replication, we needed this VM to be available and running with the same capacity as the VM in the primary region. We could have considered a smaller VM, resizing it at failover. When taking a smaller VM, keep in mind that the number of disks and their throughput is dependent on the VM type. The size of the standby database is always the same as the primary database. The disk layout should be exactly the same.

Conclusion

So, what did the customer decide? In the end, we implemented the 99.9% option. The customer was new to Azure and the 99.95% and 99.99% setups were considered too complicated. The customer wanted the migration to be as straightforward as possible. The approach taken was to first migrate to Azure and to enhance availability in a second phase. The environment will be converted to meet the 99.95% requirements in the months to come.

9.2.4 Backup and restore

It is always necessary to back up your systems, even if data is kept in three separate locations, as is the case in Azure. This also applies if you work with availability sets and zones, and if you operate primary, secondary and standby databases. Keeping different copies of your data does not protect your data from human errors such as data deletions or corruptions. Backing up and restoring SAP ASE works in the same way as it does in on-premise installations.

Our customer was using the following backup schedule:

- For the production systems they had daily database dumps which were kept for 30 days, weekly dumps which were kept for four weeks, and monthly dumps which were kept for 12 months.
- Backups were kept for 10 days for non-production systems. Non-production systems can always be rebuilt from production in worst-case scenarios.

In our customer's new environment on Azure, backups or dumps are taken to disks which are connected to two DS12v2 virtual machines (see Table 9.6).

VM	VM-Serie	Description	Size	Disk	IOPS
Database dumps	DS12v2	OS	500	P20	2300
	2vCPU/28GB	Storage	4000	2*P40	2*7500
Transaction log backups	DS12v2	OS	500	P20	2300
	2vCPU/28GB	Storage	4000	2*P40	2*7500

Table 9.6: Virtual machines and Azure Backup for storing the backup dumps

Our customer's new backup solution consists of the following building blocks (see Figure 9.5):

- There are two virtual machines, one for the database dumps and another for the transaction log backups. These virtual machines are saved by the Azure Backup Service twice a day using snapshots. These snapshots are written to Azure Blog Storage. Azure Blog Storage is a cheap storage option and is well suited for data backups and archiving.
- Daily database dumps are taken by the database to a mounted file system. The file system resides on the virtual machine dedicated to backups. For the production systems, a full database dump is taken daily. For non-production systems, full database dumps are taken weekly in combination with daily differential database dumps. There are not as many changes on non-production systems as there are on production systems. We therefore use differential backups to decrease the required disk space on the backup VM.
- For the production systems, a transaction log backup is taken to the mounted file system every 15 minutes. The file system resides in a VM dedicated to transaction log backups.

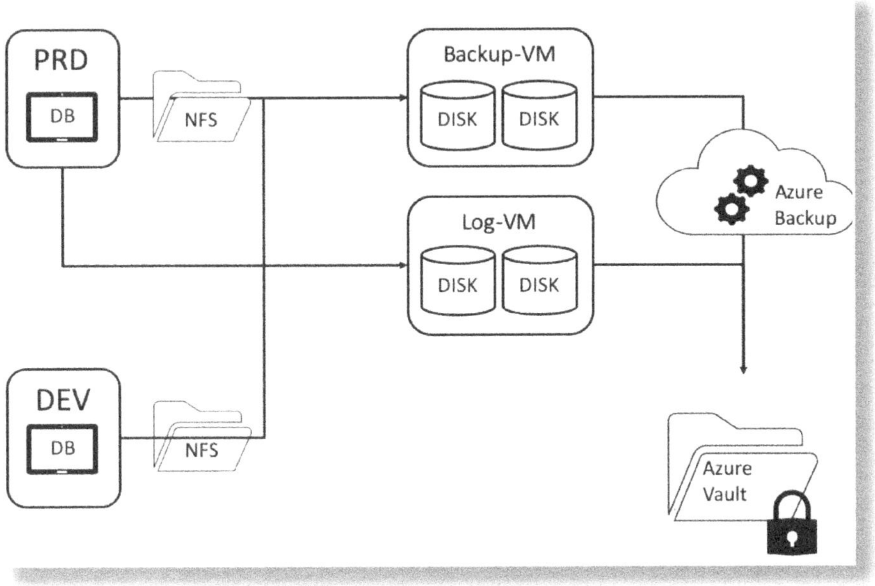

Figure 9.5: Example backup architecture using Azure Backup

10 Conclusion

A recent survey from ComputerWorld[1] revealed that 60% of North American companies rely on public cloud platforms, which is five times the amount five years prior; and 70% have already moved at least one application, or a portion of their infrastructure, to the Cloud. Another 16% plan to do so in the next 12 months, and 14% plan to move applications or infrastructure to the Cloud within the next three years.

According to Gartner[2], 55% of large enterprises will have successfully implemented an all-in cloud SaaS strategy by 2025. This figure differs depending on the source, but the trend cannot be ignored—the Cloud is coming. It is not a matter of if, but when!

When asked why this will be the case, CIOs point to the need for flexibility, agility, and scalability to accommodate fast-changing business requirements. In addition, SAP customers mention SAP HANA and S/4HANA as drivers for looking at the Cloud. The need for certified hardware is often mentioned. Acquiring and maintaining certified hardware for on-premise installations is still expensive and complex.

CIOs also focus on the importance of cost containment. In the Cloud, you pay as you go (PAYG). Resources can be upscaled and downscaled as needed. In Azure, costs are flexible and control can be very granular. In addition to PAYG, there are Reserved Instances (RIs). With RIs, you reserve a certain set of resources for one, two, or three years. RIs can reduce costs by up to 70%. Costs can be optimized by combining RI and PAYG. RIs can be used for stable loads, while PAYG can be used to intercept peaks in resource requirements (for example, adding application servers during month-end closing).

Forrester Consulting recently released a study “The Total Economic Impact of Microsoft Azure for SAP” in which they list the following benefits of the Cloud and Azure:

---

1 *https://www.computerworld.com/article/3427955/cloud-computing-trends-for-2019.html*
2 *https://www.gartner.com/imagesrv/books/cloud/cloud_strategy_leadership.pdf*

- The Cloud avoids costs for on-premise hardware. Note that the costs for on-premise hardware are not limited to the hardware itself. You also have to account for hosting, data center, cooling, and electricity.
- In the Cloud, under or overprovisioning of hardware can be avoided. Many customers overprovision hardware resources, resulting in expensive systems that are under-utilized.
- The renewal rate of hardware in the Cloud is much faster than in on-premise installations. Most customers keep their systems for three to five years. In the Cloud, the underlying hardware infrastructure is renewed at a much faster rate.
- Faster time to market. Businesses need new applications fast in order to respond to changing market requirements. In the Cloud, infrastructure is at your fingertips. Projects do not have to be halted due to a lack of resources.

The Forrester study is available at: *https://azure.microsoft.com/en-us/resources/sap-on-azure-forrester-tei/*.

SAP and Microsoft have been working together for 25 years. Microsoft runs SAP as well, and has one of the largest SAP installations on Azure.

Microsoft recently made the following announcements:

- Virtual machines with up to 6TB of memory will be available as of Q2 2019. In addition, 12TB VMs have been announced for Q3.
- As of Q4 2019, 9TB and 18TB Large Instance for SAP HANA will be available.
- There will be a beta release of the integration of Azure Backup with SAP HANA.
- There will be integration between the Azure IA and IOT solutions from the SAP Digital Platform.

According to Microsoft, more than 90% of Fortune 500 companies use Azure and SAP. In my opinion, Azure is the best choice for customers considering the Cloud thanks to its flexibility with respect to setup, configuration and administration, and the integration and support between Microsoft and SAP.

11 References

Writing a book without preparation and documentation is unwise and creates a recipe for disaster. In writing this book, many existing sources and documentation have been referenced and are listed below.

11.1 SAP support notes

SAP Notes and SAP Knowledge Base Articles (KBA) are support documents that help you find answers to questions arising from your daily work with SAP software products.

In this book, we have referenced the following SAP Notes:

- 2316233—SAP HANA on Microsoft Azure (Large Instances)
- 1928533—"SAP Applications on Azure: Supported Products and Azure VM types"
- 2039619—"SAP Applications on Microsoft Azure using the Oracle Database: Supported Products and Versions"
- 2015553—"SAP on Microsoft Azure: Support Prerequisites"
- 2233094—"DB6: SAP Applications on Azure Using IBM DB2 for Linux, UNIX, and Windows - Additional Information"
- 2191498—"SAP on Linux with Azure: Enhanced Monitoring"
- 1825774—"SAP Business Suite Powered by SAP HANA - Multi-Node Support"

The following SAP Notes are also important and should be considered when migrating to Azure:

- 2367194—"Use of Azure Premium SSD Storage for SAP RDBMS Instance"
- 171356—"SAP Software on Linux: General Information"

- 1944799—"SAP HANA Guidelines for SLES Operating System Installation"
- 2205917—"SAP HANA DB: Recommended OS Settings for SLES 12/SLES for SAP Applications 12"
- 1984787—"SUSE Linux Enterprise Server 12: Installation Notes"
- 1391070—"Linux UUID Solutions"
- 2009879—"SAP HANA Guidelines for Red Hat Enterprise Linux (RHEL) Operating System"
- 2292690—"SAP HANA DB: Recommended OS settings for RHEL 7"
- 1102124—"SAPOSCOL on Linux: Enhanced function"
- 2178632—"Key Monitoring Metrics for SAP on Microsoft Azure"

We have also made reference to the following SAP documentation and blogs:

- White paper—"Best Practice Guide - Considerations for Custom ABAP Code During a Migration to SAP HANA". This document is available at: *https://archive.sap.com/documents/docs/DOC-46714*
- Blog—"SAP S/4HANA Silent Installation", containing information on how to use the SAP Silent Installation option in an Azure context. The blog can be found at: *https://techcommunity.microsoft.com/t5/Running-SAP-Applications-on-the/SAP-S-4HANA-Silent-Installation/ba-p/711289*
- SAP landing page for the SAP OS/DB Migration Check (requires logon to SAP Support Portal): *https://support.sap.com/en/offerings-programs/support-services/os-db-migration-check.html*
- The SAP HANA Hardware Directory, available at: *https://www.sap.com/dmc/exp/2014-09-02-hana-hardware/enEN/iaas.html.*
- Blog—"Introducing Proximity Placement Groups" *https://azure.microsoft.com/en-us/blog/introducing-proximity-placement-groups*

11.2 Azure documentation

The following guides are available for SAP deployments on Azure:

- SAP HANA on Azure (Large Instances)
- SAP HANA on Azure Virtual Machines
- SAP NetWeaver and Business One on Azure Virtual Machines

The documents listed above are available via the Azure documentation portal for SAP at: *https://docs.microsoft.com/en-us/azure/virtual-machines/workloads/sap/get-started*.

Several additional references were used in writing this book:

- Azure subscription and service limits, quotas and constraints, available at: *https://docs.microsoft.com/en-us/azure/azure-subscription-service-limits*
- All virtual machines and their capabilities are listed in detail in the Azure documentation portal, which is available at: *https://docs.microsoft.com/en-us/azure/virtual-machines/windows/sizes*
- The Azure Pricing Calculator can be found at: *https://azure.microsoft.com/en-us/pricing/calculator*
- For more information on deploying MaxDB on Azure see: *https://docs.microsoft.com/en-us/azure/virtual-machines/workloads/sap/dbms_guide_maxdb*
- Detailed documentation on how to implement Oracle with VSS is available at: *https://docs.oracle.com/en/database/oracle/oracle-database/12.2/ntqrf/basic-concepts-of-database-backup-and-recovery-with-vss.html#GUID-E80A9CAC-A3BD-4C07-AD75-97FED36EB6C0*
- For more information about disaster recovery for Oracle databases in Azure, see: *https://docs.microsoft.com/en-us/azure/virtual-machines/workloads/oracle/oracle-disaster-recovery*
- SQL Server Deployment in Azure, available at: *https://docs.microsoft.com/en-us/azure/virtual-machines/workloads/sap/dbms_guide_sqlserver*

- For more information on Autoscaling Metrics please visit *https://docs.microsoft.com/en-us/azure/azure-monitor/platform/autoscale-common-metrics*

11.3 Studies and articles

Studies and articles which were referenced in this book are:

- ComputerWorld, "Cloud computing trends for 2019", available at: *https://www.computerworld.com/article/3427955/cloud-computing-trends-for-2019.html*
- Gartner study "Cloud Strategy Leadership", which can be found at: *https://www.gartner.com/imagesrv/books/cloud/cloud_strategy_leadership.pdf*
- Forrester Consulting study "The Total Economic Impact of Microsoft Azure for SAP", available at: *https://azure.microsoft.com/en-us/resources/sap-on-azure-forrester-tei/*

ESPRESSO TUTORIALS

You have finished the book.

Sign up for our newsletter!

Stay up to date!

Sign up for our newsletter for updates on new SAP book releases and exclusive discounts.

http://newsletter.espresso-tutorials.com.

A About the Authors

Bert Vanstechelman

Bert Vanstechelman is a Partner and principal technical consultant at Expertum. He has more than 20 years of experience in SAP technical consulting, covering countless SAP versions in combination with all kinds of databases and operating systems supported by SAP. Bert specializes in platform migrations, SAP release upgrades, and SAP HANA conversions. Bert is the founder of Logos Consulting, now a part of Expertum.

Bert is a member of the board of advisors of the SAP Professional Journal. He is the author of "SAP HANA Implementation Guide" and co-author of "Securing S/4HANA", both published by Espresso Tutorials. He is also the co-author, with Mark Mergaerts, of the following SAP PRESS books: "Upgrading SAP", "SAP NetWeaver Application Server Upgrade Guide", "The OS/DB Migration Project Guide", and the "mySAP ERP Upgrade Project Guide".

He can be contacted at *bert.vanstechelman@expertum.net*.

Wouter Van Ghysegem

Wouter Van Ghysegem is a creator of small press cartoons and comic books. In 2017, his creations were awarded the Willemsfonds prize. He is well known for the "Jager", "Drew and Isa" and the "Zegening der Ringen" comic books. In addition to cartoons and comic books, he works on promotional material, such as for the Bruges Beer festival. He has a master's degree in art and currently teaches art.

About Expertum

At Expertum, we offer functional and technical expertise on a broad range of SAP solutions, from S/4HANA, C/4HANA, and Analytics, to SAP Security, Solution Manager, etc. We also offer technological knowledge on how best to install, migrate, upgrade, integrate, monitor, and maintain these SAP solutions and underlying databases.

Our mission is to provide in-depth technical and functional expertise in the SAP area—to assist our customers and our implementation partners during their key projects and daily operations. We aim to establish long-term relationships in order to assist our customers today, and to continue to provide them with future-proof strategic platform and solution advice for tomorrow.

Our consultants are our most important assets. We inspire them to be the best, and we provide them with the necessary support, education, and knowledge sharing to achieve this. This approach provides our customers with focused and motivated individuals who act as trusted advisors.

We strive for continuing relationships in which we guide our customers during periods of high workload. We assist them with large implementation projects; assignments ranging from full-time, on-site presence to frequent visits. We also provide remote support, to take the burden of daily administration out of our customers' hands. Finally, in emergency situations, our consultants go the extra mile to ensure quick recovery of system infrastructure.

We strongly believe in the exchange of knowledge and information to the benefit of our consultants and our partners. In cooperation with Espresso Tutorials, we have published the following books:

- "Securing S/4HANA"
- "The SAP HANA Implementation Guide"

In cooperation with SAP PRESS, we have published the following SAP books:

- "Upgrading SAP"
- "SAP NetWeaver Application Server Upgrade Guide"
- "ERP Upgrade Project Guide"
- "The SAP OS/DB Migration Project Guide"

In addition, we advise the SAP Professional Journal on technical SAP subjects.

Expertum goes SAP HANA

From 2025, SAP solutions will only be supported on SAP HANA. Today, several SAP solutions are already only available on SAP HANA; for example, S/4HANA.

Expertum is the leader in SAP HANA implementation projects in Belgium, and the quality and experience of our certified consultants are widely acknowledged. This has been recognized by SAP Belgium on several occasions: when they awarded Expertum the SAP HANA innovation award in 2014, when they joined forces with Expertum during the "SAP HANA in the Box" campaign in 2015, and when they awarded Expertum the SAP Quality Award for the fast delivery implementation of SAP BW on HANA in 2017.

About SUSAN

The SUSAN platform is a comprehensive system for monitoring all aspects of SAP NetWeaver ABAP and SAP NetWeaver Java systems (see Figure 11.1). SUSAN has been developed by Expertum and builds on the company's extensive expertise in the field of SAP technology.

Expertum uses SAP Solution Manager, which covers a wide variety of SAP solutions as a foundation for monitoring and supporting customer systems. However, we made the conscious decision that for SAP NetWeaver systems, which are at the very heart of a company's SAP landscape, we needed more than Solution Manager could provide. The extensive experience and in-depth knowledge of Expertum consultants has resulted in the unique power and flexibility of SUSAN.

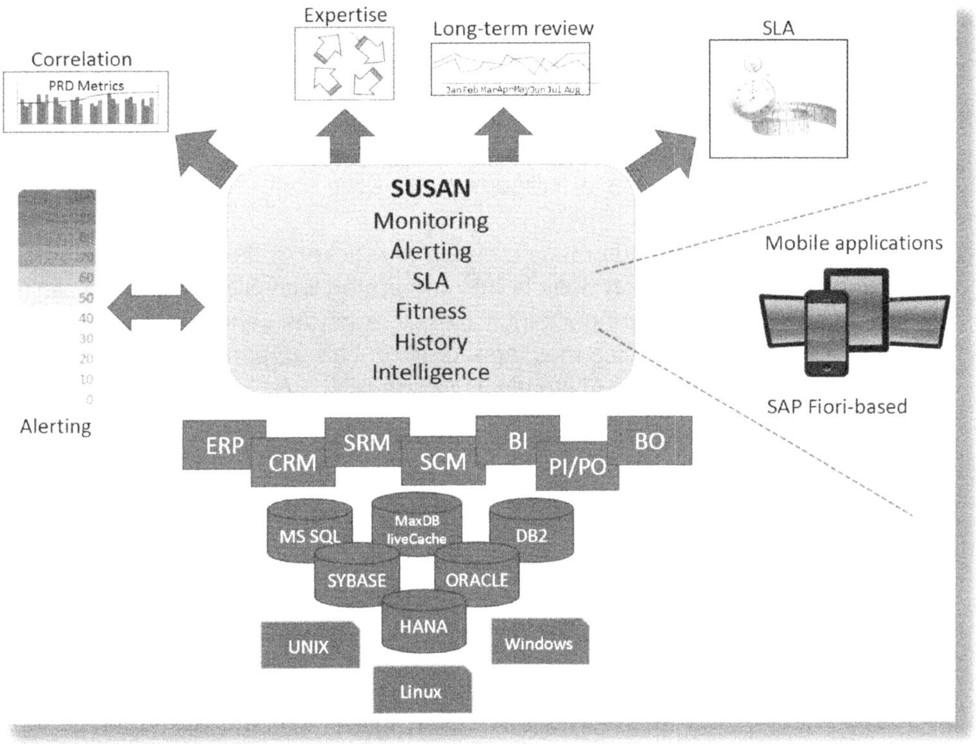

Figure 11.1: SUSAN platform

Data collection and alerts

SUSAN monitors the SAP NetWeaver system using a data collection process that is powerful and highly flexible, but has a very small footprint itself. Elements are monitored at (configurable) frequencies that take into account their criticality and their likelihood to change at short notice, with the ability to check crucial KPIs as often as once a minute.

SUSAN goes beyond the traditional traffic-light metaphor, where a monitored element is simply flagged as green (OK), yellow (warning), or red (problem). Experience shows that this is too crude a method for evaluating the status of a system, especially if, as is the case for the SAP NetWeaver system, there are a large number of monitored elements. Instead of the rudimentary red-yellow-green differentiation, SUSAN uses a sophisticated **color calculus** which takes into account not only the seriousness of the alert, but also other things such as the context in which the alert is occurring. This ensures that the status of the system is diagnosed in far more detail, and avoids issues such as **red saturation,** where, at any point in time, numerous elements are reported with a red status.

Alerts can trigger the automatic creation of a ticket in the support system (Expertum's own support desk is fully integrated with SUSAN). They can also be configured to trigger other actions, such as sending an email or transmitting a text or voice message to an on-call support engineer. Other channels into which SUSAN feeds its information are:

- a *kiosk*, which is the equivalent of the alert inbox in other products,
- a *dashboard*, which shows the status of a system or group of systems at a glance, and
- a collection of graphs and statistical reports.

Reporting

Monitoring with SUSAN does more than trigger alerts. The information collected is used to build an extensive knowledge database, which in turn serves as the basis for a set of convenient reports. The collector configuration is so flexible that you can set the frequency of each collector to as low as one minute, or as high as days or weeks. This enables you to set up a monitoring schedule that keeps a close eye on the SAP NetWeaver system and simultaneously relieves administrators of repetitive work. Here are some examples:

- The **Early Morning Report**—system administrators often verify the system every morning with time-consuming and error-prone transaction hopping. They execute transactions such as SM37, SM58, SMQR, SMQS, SM12, SM13, SM50, SM51, SM66, ST22, WE05, and many more. SUSAN automates this tedious chore by automatically generating its Early Morning Report, which is ready and waiting for the administrator at the start of the workday. Users can navigate through earlier reports, up to 14 days old, to examine how an issue has evolved over time.

- **Hourly reporting**—to follow the system status by the hour, SUSAN generates an hourly update from a full system monitoring report. The hourly updates are then made available in a time-navigable interface. Navigation through earlier reports, up to 48 hours old, is possible. In update mode, the hourly reports are continuously updated as new data from the collectors becomes available, which makes the reporting facility almost real-time.
- **High frequency monitoring**—because of SUSAN's ability to run collectors as often as once a minute, it can keep a permanent watch on critical elements of the system. This results in an immediate response—all events of interest appear in the kiosk or on the dashboard, and a support incident is generated and shows up in the reports.

In addition to its monitoring functions, SUSAN is also capable of generating a detailed system review over any requested time period (weeks, months, or years).

Customization

The design of the SUSAN collection process makes it very easy to add or enhance data collectors. Our customers have frequently benefited from this capability because we have been able to provide them with alerts within just a few days. With other products, this would have taken months, or would never have been developed at all due to the specificity of the request. Some real-life examples we have used are:

- specific monitoring of ABAP dumps triggered by custom (Z) code
- special high-priority alert if a specific group of jobs fails or does not start
- customized monitoring for critical business jobs based on the customer's internal communication procedures

- high frequency (every 2 minutes) monitoring of commercial portals (lost connection = lost sale)
- non-SAP RFC interface monitoring and availability check
- monitor mainframe file systems mounted on Windows or Unix server
- monitoring of number ranges
- monitoring of connections to non-SAP applications.

Installation and configuration

In contrast to SAP Solution Manager and most third-party monitoring products, SUSAN is extremely easy to install and maintain. The data collection uses standard functions in SAP as much as possible. Where standard functions are not available, SUSAN uses a light-weight agent installed in the monitored system; this is the only software to be installed there.

Thanks to its efficient, performance-oriented design, SUSAN has the capacity to monitor dozens or even hundreds of systems simultaneously. A new system can be added to the SUSAN watch list in a matter of minutes.

B Index

C Disclaimer

This publication contains references to the products of SAP SE.

SAP, R/3, SAP NetWeaver, Duet, PartnerEdge, ByDesign, SAP BusinessObjects Explorer, StreamWork, and other SAP products and services mentioned herein as well as their respective logos are trademarks or registered trademarks of SAP SE in Germany and other countries.

Business Objects and the Business Objects logo, BusinessObjects, Crystal Reports, Crystal Decisions, Web Intelligence, Xcelsius, and other Business Objects products and services mentioned herein as well as their respective logos are trademarks or registered trademarks of Business Objects Software Ltd. Business Objects is an SAP company.

Sybase and Adaptive Server, iAnywhere, Sybase 365, SQL Anywhere, and other Sybase products and services mentioned herein as well as their respective logos are trademarks or registered trademarks of Sybase, Inc. Sybase is an SAP company.

SAP SE is neither the author nor the publisher of this publication and is not responsible for its content. SAP Group shall not be liable for errors or omissions with respect to the materials. The only warranties for SAP Group products and services are those that are set forth in the express warranty statements accompanying such products and services, if any. Nothing herein should be construed as constituting an additional warranty.

More Espresso Tutorials Books

Dominique Alfermann, Stefan Hartmann:

Practical Guide to SAP HANA and Big Data Analytics

- SAP HANA and SAP BW/4HANA architecture concepts
- Predictive Analytics and Big Data component integration
- Recommendations for a sustainable, future-proof analytics solutions
- Organizational impact and change management

http://5179.espresso-tutorials.com

Gretchen Horn:

Practical Guide to SAP Workflow Agent Determination

- Fundamentals of SAP Business Workflow agent types and agent determination
- Example rules defined using responsibilities, ABAP, evaluation paths, organizational data, and BRF+
- Agent administration and reporting
- Deep dive workshops exploring rule definition, modeled deadlines, ad hoc agents, and release procedures

http://5200.espresso-tutorials.com

Bert Vanstechelman, Chris Walravens, Christophe Decamps

Securing SAP S/4HANA

- Effectively secure SAP S/4HANA, Fiori, and Gateway
- Privileges and roles, authentication, encryption, and monitoring
- Mobile access and SSO considerations
- Cross-system authorization concepts and implementation

http://5258.espresso-tutorials.com

Bert Vanstechelman

SAP HANA—Implementation Guide

- SAP HANA sizing, capacity planning guidelines, and data tiering
- Deployment options and data provisioning scenarios
- Backup and recovery options and procedures
- Software and hardware virtualization in SAP HANA

http://5289.espresso-tutorials.com

Made in United States
Orlando, FL
04 November 2026

90202171R00115